International Praise for
Divine Nature
A Spiritual Perspective on the Environmental Crisis

"At a time when the world's developing countries are tending to let industrial progress take over their economies oblivious to environmental destruction, *Divine Nature* comes as a welcome breath of relief. The authors have persuasively argued that a return to the original value of humanity's deep spiritual kinship with all the living things is the key to achieving a pervasive environmental consciousness ꞏꞏꞏ ultimately salvage our poisoned planet. In ꞏꞏꞏ ꞏꞏꞏ are only restating India's stand on ꞏꞏꞏ ꞏꞏꞏ is basically an attitude, to ꞏꞏꞏ ꞏꞏꞏ de towards environmeꞏꞏꞏ ꞏꞏꞏ lique amongst the comꞏꞏꞏ ꞏꞏꞏ, in turn, stems from our philꞏꞏꞏ ꞏꞏꞏ all living creatures on planet Earth ꞏꞏꞏ ꞏꞏꞏ ng them for our selfish purposes. In that respeꞏꞏꞏ ꞏꞏꞏ regard nature as divine and expect other nations of the world to do the same."

Kamal Nath
Minister, Environment & Forests, India

"In view of the crying need for excellent literature concerning the interface of spirituality and the environment, *Divine Nature* is a godsend. In addition, *Divine Nature* deserves the attention of scholars and students of religion because it is an insightful, well-researched, and in many ways very practical approach to environmental issues.

Divine Nature is a must for professors of religion like myself and for students like mine. It shows us that the apparently abstract and ethereal realm of spirituality bears upon the environment in a quite positive and practical way."

Gene C. Sager
Professor of Religious Studies and Philosophy
Palomar College, San Marcos, California

Divine
Nature

Divine Nature

A Spiritual Perspective on the Environmental Crisis

Michael A. Cremo
Mukunda Goswami
Foreword by William McDonough

THE BHAKTIVEDANTA BOOK TRUST
Los Angeles • London • Stockholm • Bombay • Sydney • Hong Kong

Readers interested in the subject matter of this book are invited to correspond with the authors at the following address:

Bhaktivedanta Book Trust
3764 Watseka Avenue
Los Angeles, CA 90034
USA
Telephone: (800) 927-4152

First printing, 1995: 5,000
Second printing, 1995: 100,000

Foreword copyright 1995 by William A. McDonough

Printed on recycled paper.

Printed in Australia

Library of Congress Cataloging in Publication Data

Cremo, Michael A., 1948-
    Divine nature : a spiritual perspective on the environmental crisis / by Michael A. Cremo and Mukunda Goswami.
        p.   cm.
    Includes bibliographical references.
    ISBN 0-89213-297 (Trade Paper), ISBN 0-89213-296-5 (Mass Market Paperback)
        1. Human ecology--Religious aspects--Hinduism.
    2. Environmental protection--Religious aspects--Hinduism.
    3. Hinduism--Doctrines.
    4. International Society for Krishna Consciousness. I. Goswami, Mukunda, 1942-   .
    BL1215.N34D37   1995   95-5867
    294.5'178362--dc20   CIP

Dedicated to our spiritual master,
His Divine Grace
A. C. Bhaktivedanta Swami Prabhupāda,
whose teachings inspired the writing of
Divine Nature

Contents

Contents

Foreword

When I was asked to write a foreword for *Divine Nature,* I felt instantly humbled. Here was a book by people for whom every daily act is expressly connected to matters of the spirit, whereas I spend much of my life absorbed in matters of commerce. But then as architects and designers, our finest work is definitely connected to the joy and spirit of the Divine, and it is indeed in nature that we find ourselves in what I call "the world of the making of things."

This was not the first time I had been asked to comment on the way we might interact with the natural world from the perspective of human industry. In 1992 the city of Hanover, Germany, asked my firm to prepare design principles for the World's Fair to be held there in the year 2000. Of all design principles, there is one that my colleagues among the indigenous peoples around the world insist is the most important: "Respect the relationships between spirit and matter." We say all design principles flow from this one; this is the source of our joy, our humanity, and also . . . our responsibility.

I have come to see the act of design itself as one of the first signals of human intention. And if the modern world of industry were being intentionally recreated on a clean slate today, it would represent a most terrifying and unnatural design assignment. Can you imagine being instructed to use human intelligence to design a system that releases billions of kilos of highly toxic material into the air, soil, and water every year? Can you imagine being instructed to create places so befouled by bad air that people fear going outdoors or need a lamp at midday to see their way? Can you imagine, on a planet whose surface is abundant with natural energy flows driven by the sun, being instructed to dig up ancient toxic materials whose very burial has allowed us to inhabit this surface, and further being told to burn them, pave with them, and allow products derived from them to persistently invade almost every living system, to the point where some species can no longer even reproduce? Can you imagine being told to use a wood whose harvest is effectively causing the genocide of a tribe of people half way around the world? One might say these instructions would be not only unethical but unintelligent. One might then conclude that these instructions could not possibly foster ethical or intelligent designs. And yet the horrifying effects mentioned above are some of the daily results of modern industrial artifice.

So if we as a civilization are to begin interacting with nature in an ethical and intelligent way, we must ask ourselves if human beings could imagine a better series of "instructions" and design assignments to which we can apply our unusual skills. This is clearly a central question inherent in the issues being raised by *Divine Nature*: how do we find, and come to peace with, our place in the natural world?

From my design perspective, it is obvious that we should be working with, and not against, nature's own design principles. For example, nature barely entertains the concept of waste: one thing's waste is another thing's food. Everything moves in cycles: cradle to cradle, not cradle to grave, as modern industrial protocols would ask us to believe. Nature operates on "current income"—it does not mine or extract energy from the past, it does not use its capital reserves, and it does not borrow from the future. Nature is an extraordinarily complex yet elegant and efficient system for creating and cycling nutrients, so economical that modern manufacturing methods pale in comparison. And nature loves diversity: everything is different from everything else, but everything has its place.

Today politicians, scientists, and business people are becoming aware of the critical importance of biodiversity; they are recognizing the richness of all living systems and the infinitely complex interdependencies within and between them. They are beginning to see that everything is indeed connected to everything else, and they are becoming aware of an impending crisis. Some see grave dangers, others opportunities lost. I was told a story recently about an eminent naturalist who went to see the Chief of Staff of a U.S. President to explain the importance of a proposed international biodiversity convention. Apparently the politician, who was trained as an engineer, responded in effect: "Oh, I see, you're talking about an Endangered Species Act for the whole world, and it sounds like the Devil is in the details." To which the scientist responded, "No, sir, God is in the details." Einstein is credited with noticing that almost no problem can be solved by the same consciousness that created it.

The change in consciousness needed now must be deep, informed, and integrated with a great deal of ancient wisdom. As this book explains, we must be humble enough to recognize that those who came before us have pondered many of our concerns.

In the world of design, some of the proposed solutions may reflect the same linear consciousness that got us to our present state. A single example may suffice. In many places in the world, designers are looking toward the production of biomass to produce energy—growing grasses, trees, etc., specifically to be burned to create heat and electricity. The problem is that while the system may be what engineers call CO_2 neutral—i.e., it releases only as much carbon dioxide as was absorbed by the plants as they grew to maturity—it represents a linear design that focuses on solar energy alone. Because the system does not close the natural nutrient or water cycles of the soils being depleted, it can reduce biodiversity. The biomass is seen as carbohydrates replacing hydrocarbons, and water is seen in chemical terms, as H_2O, and not as part of a larger living organism. Outside nutrients such as mineral fertilizers must be imported to maintain energy production levels because many of the soil-nurturing materials have gone up in smoke. Such a system of energy production is the large-scale equivalent of burning wood to boil water, which really makes sense only where you have a lot of wood and a few people, like a forest tribe. But right now the planet is experiencing a dramatic loss in the number of trees and a sobering increase in the number of people. So if the current system of getting energy by burning either biomass or fossil fuel is continued, it is only a matter of time before population pressure will strain the system to its breaking point.

I helped design villages like those described in this book, villages where people are elegantly and efficiently harvesting solar energy in all its myriad forms: as food, in low-temperature thermal collection, in the form of animal husbandry, and as cooking gas from "digested" dung and biomass. Nutrients are returned to the soil, maintaining an endless cycle of use and refreshment. The intent is clear: nothing is lost and nothing is wasted and nothing needs to be imported from far away. This is the model to which we must turn our attention if we are to create both ethical and intelligent designs.

As designers, we are using these models to inform every element of our work, from products to buildings to, yes, even cities. We are designing products that can be safely composted at the end of their useful life, others that go back to solar-powered manufactories to be completely reused over and over, without any waste or release of materials in the cycle, and we are also developing the concept of zero-emission industries within "industrial ecologies." Essentially we are trying to imagine the next industrial revolution—one where there are small-scale, linked, local enterprises, where prosperity is measured by the health of the economic and ecological system in terms of the quality of all life, and where productivity is measured not by how many resources are used up by how few people but by how few resources are used up by how many people.

Now that I live in Charlottesville, Virginia, I often think

of Thomas Jefferson, who designed the house in which my family lives. He was clearly a person who understood design as a signal of intention. He also wrote in his Declaration of Independence of the right to life, liberty, and the pursuit of happiness, free from remote tyranny. There is no question in my mind that if Mr. Jefferson were alive today he would be calling for "A Declaration of Interdependence," and the forms of remote tyranny concerning him would include the depositing of pollutants into the air, water, and soil. In 1789 he wrote the following in a letter to James Madison: "The earth belongs . . . to the living: . . . Then no man can, by natural right, oblige the lands he occupied or the persons who succeed him in that occupation, to the payment of debts contracted by him. For if he could, he might, during his own life, eat up the use of the lands for several generations to come, and then the lands would belong to the dead, and not to the living, . . . No generation can contract debts greater than may be paid during the course of its own existence."

This is one of the organizing concepts being talked about today under the heading "sustainable development," and it is indeed wonderful to see people worldwide recognizing that their common security lies in embracing this principle. But even sustainable development has the ring of anthropocentric tyranny, remote from the rest of nature. It often speaks of resource flows but barely touches the most ineffable of relationships, which are also the most human—the relationships between spirit, matter, and place. These intertwined relationships still seem to be the least understood and most resisted by an industrialized world whose guiding principle has been dominion over nature and whose stewardship of the natural world is often patronizing. We must learn again of our kinship with the natural world and enjoy its message, which tells of the value of all life and the rightful place of humans as part of it.

This book, *Divine Nature,* reminds us that we must learn again to live within the laws of nature and find the means of expressing our human intention as interdependent actors, aware that we are at the mercy of sacred forces larger than ourselves, and aware also that we must obey the laws governing these forces in order to honor the sacred in each other, and in all things. It instructs us correctly: we must come to peace with and accept our place in the natural world in order to enjoy the spirit of belonging to the earth firsthand.

©William McDonough,
Author of *The Hanover Principle*
Dean of Architecture
University of Virginia

Introduction and Acknowledgments

In the early morning, Mukunda Goswāmī and I walk down a narrow, dusty, tree-lined road in the rural town of Vṛndāvana, in northern India. Monkeys scamper along the tops of stone walls, and peacocks cry from their perches high in the trees. In this timeless place of pilgrimage, a center of Kṛṣṇa worship for thousands of years, the melodious chanting of Kṛṣṇa *mantras* floats from a nearby temple. Vṛndāvana, a town of 50,000 people, has 5,000 Kṛṣṇa temples. According to many sacred texts, it is the earthly manifestation of Kṛṣṇa's eternal spiritual abode.

A farmer drives toward us on a simple wooden cart pulled by a bullock. The wheels rumble lightly over the road, and some small bells on the animal jingle. Suddenly, another farmer comes from the opposite direction, driving a big tractor, which pulls a big metal trailer full of bricks. The passing tractor's engine assaults our ears with its pounding roar, and the trailer clangs and rattles harshly. Our nostrils are filled with a pungent mixture of dust and exhaust. Peaceful, meditative Vṛndāvana has been invaded by a symbol of an alien way of life.

The simple bullock cart performs the same function as the tractor and trailer. The cart is made of locally available wood, and the bullock who pulls it was born from other bullocks in the neighborhood. He eats only hay and other vegetable matter. But the tractor and trailer require a huge worldwide arrangement of mines, factories, and refineries. And it is this huge arrangement that is generating most of the environmental problems we face.

Mukunda Goswāmī and I came to Vṛndāvana in October and November of 1993 to complete the final draft of *Divine Nature,* a book that gives a Vṛndāvana perspective on the world's environmental crisis. As devotees of Kṛṣṇa, we came to seek inspiration in Vṛndāvana's unique spiritual atmosphere and to experience firsthand a way of life that, despite the occasional loud tractor, still harmonizes with the natural rhythms and movements of mother nature.

On the surface, Vṛndāvana is not without environmental problems. The sewage system is inadequate. There are unsightly piles of garbage along some of the pilgrimage paths. Nevertheless, Vṛndāvana life points the way to a more healthy planet.

Many have suggested that the environmental crisis is a crisis of the human spirit, which has become infected with too much material acquisitiveness. Centers of spiritual culture such as Vṛndāvana offer us the chance to cleanse our souls of superfluous desires, the chance to concentrate on developing the deeper purposes of human life. And in Vṛndāvana we also find a way of life that supports this inner journey of enlightenment. Most food is produced nearby, homes are built of locally available materials, and draft animals provide power for tilling and transportation. Although many elements of modern technology have entered Vṛndāvana, the basic way of life is still simple yet rich in its spiritual dimensions.

In *Divine Nature,* we summarize the world's environmental problems. Then we review attempts to solve these problems by material means. Most of these solutions involve end-of-the-pipeline efforts to control pollution after it has been produced. We conclude, as have many other thoughtful people, that these efforts, although well meaning, will not produce the desired result. The real key is reducing the material desires that fuel the industrial complex that produces the pollutants that are destroying the environment. In other words, reducing pollution in the environment means reducing pollution of the human spirit.

We need to see the world and our very selves in a new light. Rampant material desires are the natural result of a mechanistic scientific worldview that defines humans as biological machines that have arisen by chance in a cosmos devoid of divine guidance and purpose. A new science that recognizes the reality of spiritual personhood is required.

Our vision of spiritual personhood extends to all living creatures. This is another aspect of Vṛndāvana life—respect for all God's creatures. Such respect can have important environmental benefits. The meat industry is one of the biggest sources of pollution. Therefore, the growing numbers of people adopting vegetarian diets are directly helping solve many environmental problems.

In *Divine Nature,* we also talk about the law of *karma* as one of the hidden causes underlying the planetary crisis.

A new vision of reality leads inevitably to a new way of living. Many visionaries have said that the postindustrial way of life will involve a return to small-scale rural communities, where spiritual values are cultivated side by side with fruits, grains, and vegetables. It would be a world of sustainable, livable towns and villages rather than uninhabitable urban jungles and sterile suburbs.

With over forty rural communities on five continents, the International Society for Krishna Consciousness is part of the widening circle of organizations and individuals who are taking practical steps to implement sustainable living.

Here in Vṛndāvana, Mukunda Goswāmī and I find ourselves constantly reminded, by the literature, art, and architecture of bygone centuries, that the true environment of the soul lies in the eternal Vṛndāvana of the spiritual world. As perceived by great transcendentalists in their highest spiritual visions, this ever-existing realm of Kṛṣṇa is one of unsurpassed natural beauty.

The purpose of human life, we learn from past sages, is to make this temporary and imperfect world as much like the Vṛndāvana of the spiritual world as possible. Mukunda Goswāmī and I see *Divine Nature* as a step in this direction.

For his help with *Divine Nature,* from beginning to end, we thank Advaitacandra Dāsa. The cover design is the work of Yamaraja Dāsa. Arcita dāsa, Bhakti Vaidurya Madhava

Maharaja, Draviḍa Dāsa, Yasodāmayī Devi Dāsī, Devaprastha Dāsa, Haladhara Devi Dasi, Kṛṣṇa Prīya Dāsī, and Jāhnavi Dāsī also helped in the production of this book. Finally, we express our eternal gratitude to our beloved spiritual master, His Divine Grace A. C. Bhaktivedanta Swami Prabhupāda, by whose teachings we were inspired to write *Divine Nature*.

Michael A. Cremo
(Drutakarmā Dāsa)
Vṛndāvana, India
November 5, 1993

1
A Planet in Trouble

*"The environment is burning in a hundred, in a thousand
places worldwide. But there is no fire escape here, no 'out,'
no other solution than a shift in knowing who we are."*[1]

Jim Nollman
Spiritual Ecology

About sixty miles southwest of Melbourne, Australia,
in rolling hills studded with gum trees, lies New
Nandagram, an environmentally aware community of
the International Society for Krishna Consciousness. Gokula
Dāsa, the development director of New Nandagram, is supervising the planting of trees along the border of the property.
They will not only be aesthetically pleasing but will also provide extra forage for the community's dairy cows. Expressing
his concern about degradation of the planet's ecosystem,
Gokula Dāsa says, "There is a sanctity about the earth. Even
lifelong urban dwellers are revolted by lakes of oil, stacks of
crunched automobiles, unclean air, stinking sewage systems,
dying forests, ugly garbage dumps, and unswimmable lakes
and rivers."

But what's the cause of this? "A polluted environment,"
says Gokula, "grows out of polluted consciousness. It's like
Gandhi said—there's enough on earth for everyone's need but
not for everyone's greed. We're trying to run things on that
basis at New Nandagram. We have a plan for providing all of
our residents' needs in a sustainable way. And that takes some
careful decision-making about what we really need to live happily and peacefully. It all comes down to accepting a simpler
and more natural way of life."

1

Unfortunately, a simpler way of life proceeds from different systems of values than most people hold. In both "developed" and "undeveloped" regions of the world, humanity is seeking constant improvement in personal comforts, entertainment, and personal wealth. This quest seldom has discernible limitations. People seem to have a relentless, almost unconscious drive to have and enjoy more than they really need.

Writing for the *London Observer* in 1972, Arnold Toynbee described the cause of what he called "the world's malady" as spiritual. "We are suffering," he wrote, "from having sold our souls to the pursuit of maximizing material wealth, a pursuit which is spiritually wrong and practically unattainable. We have to recognize our objective and to change it."

Many people are seeking such change. Gokula Dāsa and other members of the International Society for Krishna Consciousness (ISKCON) have chosen to explore alternative worldviews and life-styles based on an ancient wisdom that offers long-term solutions to the seemingly intractable problems of the environment.

Although most members of ISKCON live in cities, they still embrace the concept of "simple living and high thinking." But a significant number are now living in dozens of intentional rural communities throughout the world, where they practice a lifestyle of voluntary restraint based on spiritual values. Concern for the environment is a natural part of these communities.

In the hills of the Atlantic Forest region of Brazil's São Paulo province, Guru Dāsa, development director of the Hare Kṛṣṇa farm community, supervises the planting of crops that stem erosion on deforested hills, winning praise from local environmentally-minded officials. At the Hare Kṛṣṇa farm community of Gītā-Nāgarī in rural Pennsylvania, Sītā Dāsī trains a young ox to respond to her simple voice commands. When grown, the ox will help plow the fields, freeing the community from dependence on tractors. In the former Soviet Union, some Hare Kṛṣṇa members leave the food and housing shortages in the cities to start self-sufficient farm communities in the countryside. In England, Ranchor Dāsa submits a proposal to the Worldwide Fund for Nature for reforesting India's Vṛndāvana district, an area sacred to worshipers of Kṛṣṇa for thousands of years. The project is approved, with work now underway.

But there is lots of work yet to be done. Living in all parts of the world, the men, women, and children of the International Society for Krishna Consciousness are in a good position to witness firsthand the environmental crises now facing our planet. We have experienced the choking air pollution in Mexico, the deadly aftermath of the Chernobyl accident in Ukraine, the destruction of the rain forests in Brazil, the death of Swedish lakes from acid rain, and the horror of the chemical disaster in Bhopal, India. Wherever we look, we see a planet in trouble, a planet in need of spiritual healing. It is not difficult to identify greed as a root cause of pollution as we briefly survey the world's ecological predicament.

Wildlife

Unrestricted hunting of animals for food, fur, or fun is threatening the existence of many species. About 1,000 are officially recognized as endangered.

For example, during the 1980s, the number of African elephants shrank from 1.5 million to 600,000.[2] In October 1989, in an effort to stop the killing of elephants, the Convention on International Trade in Endangered Species voted to ban the trading of ivory.

Rain Forests

Rain forests are victims of the lumber and meat industries. Millions of acres are cleared and stripped annually to graze cattle

People Working for Change

Guru Dāsa

Though publicized far less than the rape of the Amazon Forest, ecological decay in the Atlantic Forest region of eastern Brazil deeply concerns national legislators and environmentalists. Sprawling across 321 lush, tropical acres in this forest is the community of Nova Gokula. Established in 1979, this settlement of 140 residents lies 114 miles northeast of São Paulo at 2,100 feet above sea level.

Officials from the nearby city of Pindamonhangaba show support for Nova Gokula because the residents conserve the region's wildlife, soil, and flora. A credo of "simple living and high thinking" and a 150-acre parcel dedicated to total self-sufficiency reinforce Mayor Vito Lerario's faith in the settlement as a sustainable ecosystem.

The emergence of Nova Gokula is intimately connected with the life and vision of Gilmar dos Santos, born in 1954 in Itajai, in the Brazilian state of Santa Catarina. After much soul-searching, dos Santos declined a major promotion from his employer, a national oil firm, opting instead to go back to basics and live off the land. In 1975, he and his wife Haldira bought a small, isolated Santa Catarina farm, where they began to realize at least one aspect of a long-cherished dream—to live independent of a petroleum-based economy.

But dos Santos was also a spiritual seeker, eagerly studying the philosophy of Kṛṣṇa consciousness. In 1979, he learned of Nova Gokula, a Hare Krsna community to the north, which was interested in new members committed to both spiritual life and rural self-sufficiency.

On his first visit, he noted the group's simplicity, purity, and determination. The dos Santoses joined the community in 1979, seizing what they saw as a rare opportunity to continue financial independence and develop spiritual consciousness at the same time.

From the very start, Gilmar found himself remarkably at home in Nova Gokula. He even helped shape its goal: to establish a community patterned after those described in the teachings of Vedic wisdom from ancient India. The Vedic system encompasses an agrarian, decentralized economic base and emphasizes cow protection and ox power.

Soon, Gilmar and Haldira accepted formal initiation into Kṛṣṇa consciousness as Guru Dāsa and Devahūti Devī Dāsī. Guru Dāsa, Nova Gokula's director of planning, established a community board, which evolved into a committed close-knit group dedicated to achieving Nova Gokula's goals according to a planned timetable.

Following Vedic standards, he trains oxen that work the fields and transport goods across varied terrain.

The emerging centerpiece of Nova Gokula, the Vedic Village, was carefully designed by Guru Dāsa and his community think tank. Governed by a charter and by-laws, it comprises 150 acres set apart for complete self-sufficiency. The small group now living there plans to produce its own cloth, shoes, paper, fuel, and castor oil for lamps. Guru Dāsa is confident the sector will prosper, unaided by motors, petroleum, electricity, or modern communications.

The village will sustain itself in part by bartering surplus agricultural and cottage-industry products, as this is within the scope of the Vedic model of self-sufficiency.

In 1985, Guru Dāsa managed Nova Gokula's host role for the ninth annual Alterative Communities' National Encounter. More than 3,000 visitors from 42 organizations took part. A main topic of the week-long convention was the community itself.

for meat production and to grow billions of tons of soy that is exported to feed beef cattle.

The world's rain forests occupy 3.5 million square miles, about the size of the United States, including Alaska and Hawaii. We lose about 45,000 square miles a year,[3] an area about the size of Nicaragua. At that rate, all the rain forests will be gone in about 80 years.

Besides the tropical forests, other forests throughout the world are also in danger. Jose Lutzenberger, Brazil's secretary for the environment, said that if the United States, Canada, Sweden, and Russia continue chopping down their remaining primeval forests, "the results could be just as devastating for the global ecosystem as the destruction of rain forests in Africa or tropical forests in New Guinea—and should be condemned by international public opinion."[4]

Soil Loss

Among the primary causes of topsoil loss is the big-business single-crop method of farming. This involves intensive use of fertilizers that leach and otherwise devitalize soil.

In the United States, beautifully red, perfectly round, and uniformly sized tomatoes sit in even rows in thousands of supermarket displays. These tomatoes often have very thick skins, and their insides are made up of an almost tasteless red pulp. But because they have enticing product names, look attractive, and feel firm, they command high prices. Their thick skins enable them to withstand fast-moving harvesting machines and all the subsequent dumping and packing operations that help make the massive quick-pick-and-pack techniques profitable. Unfortunately, this type of factory farming tends to destroy topsoil quickly. Since 1950 the world has lost about one-fifth of its topsoil from agricultural lands.[5]

Trash

Mountains of rubbish have become symbolic of people who

have more than they need. This is especially true in the industrialized nations, where the typical resident uses 10 times more steel, 12 times more fuel, and 15 times more paper than a typical resident of the developing nations [6]

Leaders in so-called underdeveloped countries are therefore sometimes irritated when ecologists from developed countries attempt to impose restrictions on their industrial growth in the name of preserving the environment.

Toxic Waste

Exotic chemicals such as dioxins and PCBs are not the only source of danger. Common heavy metals like lead, chromium, mercury, nickel, and cadmium all have poisonous effects on humans. For example, lead, found in old house paint and water pipes, is known to cause anemia, decreased intelligence, and other side effects on children. When trash is burned, poisonous heavy metals go into the air, and when trash is buried in landfills, the heavy metals often migrate into drinking-water supplies.

In 1980, the United States Environmental Protection Agency (EPA) set up a "Superfund" for cleaning up the country's most hazardous toxic waste sites. As of 1990, 1,218 sites had been designated for top-priority clean-up, but only thirty-five sites had been cleaned up and removed from the list.

Another problem with the chemical industry is the occurrence of major accidents. In 1985, a valve broke at the Union Carbide chemical plant at Bhopal, India, allowing 30 tons of lethal methyl isocyanate gas to escape. Over 2,000 people living nearby were killed, and another 17,000 received permanent injuries.[7] Such dangers compel us to question just how much industry we really need in order to function as human beings and live happily.

Toxic Trade

In August 1986, the city of Philadelphia (U.S.A.) loaded

15,000 tons of toxic ash from its trash incineration plant onto an oceangoing freighter, the *Khian Sea*. This ship spent 18 months in the Caribbean, looking unsuccessfully for a place to dump its dangerous cargo. Five continents and three name changes later, the ship allegedly found a place to legitimately offload the toxic ash, but Greenpeace says it was actually dumped illegally in the Indian Ocean in November of 1988.[8]

The reason Philadelphia had to export its ash was difficulty in finding places to dispose of it in the United States. Many European cities experience the same problem.

The U. S. and Europe are therefore engaging in the questionable practice of exporting toxic waste to developing nations, where there is far less public knowledge about (and hence less opposition to) toxic waste dumping.

Pesticides

To keep profit margins high, factory farming routinely uses chemical pesticides to protect crops from insects and animals. The many good biological, nonchemical, and nontoxic methods are seldom used. The pesticide industry vigorously markets its products and promotes vast savings for growers.

The dangers of pesticides have become well known in the industrialized countries. Many have banned the use of certain kinds, but these very same pesticides are still manufactured and exported to other countries.

For example, one-quarter of the pesticides exported by U.S. companies cannot be sold in the U.S. for any purpose.[9] Ironically, agricultural products sprayed with banned pesticides return to the U.S., which imports about 25% of all the fruits and vegetables its population consumes.

Children are at special risk. They have smaller bodies than adults and tend to eat more fresh fruits and vegetables. Therefore they are exposed to a much higher concentration of cancer-causing pesticides—about 4 times more than adults.[10]

Nuclear Waste and Accidents

The most toxic waste is nuclear waste, and its safe disposal is a problem that has yet to be solved. Nuclear plants in the United States are holding in temporary storage over 15,000 metric tons of high-level waste, which will remain harmful to human beings for about 250,000 years.[11]

Accidents are another problem. On April 26, 1986, the Chernobyl nuclear power plant in Ukraine exploded, releasing radioactive materials into the environment. Officials said 2 men died in the initial blast, and 29 firefighters were killed while trying to control the blaze. Hundreds of workers and firefighters were hospitalized, and about 135,000 people who lived within a 20-mile radius of the Chernobyl reactor were evacuated. Fallout from the reactor explosion blanketed much of Europe.

In the spring of 1991, the *Economist* magazine reported: "Vladimir Chernousenko, the scientific director of the 20-mile exclusion zone around the reactor, claims that the number of immediate Chernobyl deaths—still officially listed as 31—in fact could total as many as 7,000."[12]

Reactors in the United States are said to be safer than the Chernobyl reactor, but in 1985 American reactors were shut down for emergencies 765 times. Eighteen of the shutdowns were made in connection with serious accidents.[13] The situation could be much worse in other countries.

The most serious nuclear power plant accident in the United States occurred in 1979, when a reactor at the Three Mile Island plant in Pennsylvania partially melted down, releasing dangerously radioactive materials into the atmosphere.

Water Pollution

The most spectacular kind of water pollution involves massive oil-drilling mishaps. A 1979 accident at Ixtoc I, an exploratory well in the Gulf of Mexico, spilled 140 million gallons, covering 10% of the Gulf.

Transporting oil is also dangerous. In an average year, accidents dump about 120 million gallons of oil into the sea. But "roughly six times more oil gets into the ocean simply through routine flushing of carrier tanks, runoff from streets, and other everyday consequences of motor vehicle use," says Marcia D. Lowe of the World Watch Institute.[16]

Much life on earth depends on fresh water, and it is becoming increasingly contaminated not only by the oil industry but also by the manufacturing and meat-packing industries. About 1.75 billion of the world's people have inadequate or contaminated drinking water.[17]

Air Pollution

Most of our exposure to toxins comes from the air.[18] While we drink 2 quarts of water per day, we breathe 15 to 20 thousand quarts of air. Motor vehicles are the world's biggest source of air pollution.

A study by the World Health Organization and the United Nations Environment Program shows that two-thirds of the world's urban population live with polluted air.[19] "Anyone living in Bombay, India, is breathing air that contains pollutants equivalent to smoking ten cigarettes a day," says Lester Brown of the Worldwatch Institute.[20]

In Athens, studies have shown that the death rate is six times higher on days of heavy air pollution than on clear days. Air pollution and acid rain are also corroding famous monuments in this historic city. The Acropolis has suffered more damage in the past 25 years than in the past 2,500 years.[21]

Acid Rain

Sulfur dioxide, from factories that burn coal and oil, and nitrogen oxides, from motor vehicles, are the main causes of acid rain. Some acid rain results naturally from chemicals entering the air from volcanoes and forest fires, but our industrial civilization makes it much worse. In many places, the rain is as acid as lemon juice and in some places like battery acid.[22] Acid rain kills crops and trees, kills fish and other kinds of aquatic life in lakes, and corrodes buildings and statues.

Global Warming

Carbon dioxide makes up only .03 per cent of the atmosphere, but it is extremely important. Scientists say it traps heat that otherwise would escape into space. This greenhouse effect keeps the earth's climate from becoming uncomfortably cold.

Carbon dioxide is a natural product of organic decay and animal respiration. But industry has poured additional carbon dioxide into the air, causing potentially dangerous increases in the earth's temperature.

About 75% of the carbon dioxide entering the atmosphere each year comes from the burning of fossil fuels in factories and motor vehicles.[23] Another 20% comes from deliberate burning of forests as a method of land clearing.[24]

United Nations studies show that a warming climate could raise sea levels, which are already rising, as much as 2 meters over the next century. If sea levels rise 1 meter, this could submerge 5 million square kilometers of lowlands. These lowlands are now inhabited by one billion people and include one-third of the world's cropland.[25]

Not everyone agrees with such doomsday scenarios. But among scientists who have thrashed out the pros and cons of the issue for years, the consensus is that global warming is a fact and that rising sea levels remain a threat.

CFCs and the Ozone Layer

In 1974, F. Sherwood Rowland, a chemist at the University of California at Irvine, and Mario J. Molina, a graduate student, published a study in *Nature* showing that chlorofluorocarbons (chemicals used in aerosols, solvents, and refrigeration) destroy ozone.

Ozone in the upper atmosphere shields life on earth from the harmful effects of ultraviolet rays. Exposure to more intense ultraviolet radiation shortens the time for burning and blistering of human skin, increases the incidence of skin cancer, and causes cataracts. Excess ultraviolet radiation can also harm plant and animal life, including marine plankton, which plays an important role in the marine food cycle.

Environmental Warfare

The Gulf War of 1991 added a new dimension to the world's environmental problems. It appears that Iraq took certain actions that can be characterized as environmental warfare. Millions of gallons of oil from Kuwaiti fields were apparently deliberately released into the Persian Gulf, perhaps as a defense against amphibious assault, or perhaps as a means of crippling Saudi Arabia's water desalinization plants. Also, hundreds of oil wells were set ablaze, releasing clouds of black smoke that turned day into night over much of Kuwait. The effects of the smoke were felt over much of the Middle East and southern Asia.

Looking Ahead

Finding themselves in a world beset with the above-mentioned environmental problems, the members of the International Society for Krishna Consciousness are exploring ways to remedy them. Recognizing that environmental crisis stems from a crisis in consciousness, we are advocating a spiritual vision of the universe as the key to bringing our planet to a more healthy condition.

Positive change also involves voluntary simplicity. The ultimate result could be a less industrialized society, wherein all human beings can live more naturally and peacefully. To people blinded by shortsighted greed, such societal transformation may appear extreme. But those who can appreciate the spiritual wisdom that guided past civilizations will find it desirable.

2
Meat and the Environment

"*By eliminating beef from the human diet, our species takes a significant step toward a new species consciousness, reaching out in a spirit of shared partnership with the bovine, and, by extension, other sentient creatures with whom we share the earth.*"[1]

Jeremy Rifkin
Beyond Beef

Killing animals for food, fur, leather, and cosmetics is one of the most environmentally destructive practices taking place on the earth today. The Kṛṣṇa consciousness movement's policies of protecting animals, especially cows, and broadly promoting a spiritual vegetarian diet could—if widely adopted—relieve many environmental problems.

These policies are rooted in the following philosophical and functional principles:

1. Humans should not slaughter animals for food. They should be as compassionate to cows and other farm animals as they are to their pet dogs and cats. Nonviolence extended beyond human society is known as *ahiṁsā*, an ancient Vedic principle still practiced in some parts of the world.

2. Cows are the most valuable animals to human society. They give us fuel, fertilizer, power (for tilling, transport, grinding, and irrigating), milk and milk products, and leather (after natural death).

3. The killing of animals violates karmic laws, creating collective and individual reactions in human society.

4. Well-documented medical studies show that flesh-eating

13

is harmful to health.

5. Mass animal-killing for food and fashion erodes compassion, reducing respect for all kinds of life, including that of humans.

6. Meat diets are more expensive than nonmeat diets.

7. If the world switched to a nonmeat diet, it could radically increase its food output and save millions of people from hunger, starvation, and death.

8. Massive animal slaughter is destroying the environment. We shall now document this destruction, keeping in mind that it amounts to violence against the earth. It also has karmic consequences.

The meat industry is linked to deforestation, desertification, water pollution, water shortages, air pollution, and soil erosion. Neal D. Barnard, president of the Physicians Committee for Responsible Medicine (U.S.A.), therefore says, "If you're a meat eater, you are contributing to the destruction of the environment, whether you know it or not. Clearly the best thing you can do for the Earth is to not support animal agriculture."[2]

And Jeremy Rifkin warns in his widely read book *Beyond Beef*: "Today, millions of Americans, Europeans, and Japanese are consuming countless hamburgers, steaks, and roasts, oblivious to the impact their dietary habits are having on the biosphere and the very survivability of life on earth. Every pound of grain-fed flesh is secured at the expense of a burned forest, an eroded rangeland, a barren field, a dried-up river or stream, and the release of millions of tons of carbon dioxide, nitrous oxide, and methane into the skies."[3]

Forest Destruction

According to *Vegetarian Times,* half of the annual destruction of tropical rain forests is caused by clearing land for beef cattle ranches.[4] Each pound of hamburger made from Central American or South American beef costs about 55 square feet of rain forest vegetation.[5]

In the United States, about 260 million acres of forest have been cleared for a meat-centered diet. Each person who becomes a vegetarian saves one acre of trees per year.[6]

About 40% of the land in the Western United States is used for grazing beef cattle. This has had a detrimental effect on wildlife. Fencing has forced deer and antelope out of their natural habitats.[7]

Agricultural Inefficiency

About half the world's grain is consumed by animals that are later slaughtered for meat.[8] This is a very inefficient process. It takes 16 pounds of grain and soybeans to produce 1 pound of feedlot beef.[9] If people were to subsist on grains and other vegetarian foods alone, this would put far less strain on the earth's agricultural lands. About 20 vegetarians can be fed on the land that it takes to feed 1 meat eater.

Eighty per cent of the corn raised in the United States is fed to livestock, as well as 95% of the oats. Altogether, 56% of all agricultural land in the United States is used for beef production.[10] If all of the soybeans and grain fed yearly to U.S. livestock were set aside for human consumption, it would feed 1.3 billion people.

Soil Erosion and Desertification

Overgrazing and the intensive production of feed grain for cattle and other meat animals results in high levels of soil erosion. According to Alan B. Durning of the World Watch Institute (1986), one pound of beef from cattle raised on feedlots represents the loss of 35 pounds of topsoil.[11] Over the past few centuries, the United States has lost about two-thirds of its topsoil.

People Working for Change

Yamunā Devī

"If Americans reduced their meat intake by only 10%, 60 million people in the world could be fed," says Washington, D.C., resident Yamunā Devī. "That's especially significant when you consider that every year 20 million die of malnutrition."

When she's not writing recipes for the *Washington Post*, teaching cooking classes, or making public appearances, she's writing vegetarian cookbooks. In 1988, her *Lord Krishna's Cuisine* became the International Association of Cooking Professionals (IACP) "Best Cookbook of the Year," the only time this honor went to a book of non-Western cookery. Published in several countries, the book has become a classic of its genre. It evolved from Yamunā's more than 25 years as a lacto-vegetarian and practitioner of Kṛṣṇa consciousness. A second book, *Yamunā's Table*, has also become a steady seller.

"There's a spiritual dimension to vegetarianism that sees the world as a living planet in which all species are interdependent," says Yamunā.

"People are beginning to understand that proper vegetarian eating is better for their health. But when I explain the callousness of the meat industry and what it's doing to our environment, it penetrates to their conscience. What I call spiritual vegetarianism can be one of the most positive approaches to avoid ecological disaster."

America has lost two-thirds of its topsoil to date, she explains, adding that such erosion currently amounts to 4 million acres per year, 85% of which comes from raising animals for food.

Other facts in Yamunā's compilation:

- Half the world's destruction of tropical rain forests is directly linked with livestock enterprises, including hamburger chains;
- At present depletion rates, all rain forests will disappear from Central and South America by the year 2010;
- 1,000 species become extinct each year due to rain forest destruction.

A meat-centered diet, she points out, is nutritionally inefficient and agriculturally wasteful. Grain cycled through farm animals loses 90% of its protein. Eighty per cent of the corn and 95% of the oats grown in the U.S. are eaten by livestock. It takes 16 pounds of grain and soybeans to produce a pound of beef.

Yamunā is deeply concerned about meat's effect on water supplies, especially in technologically developed countries. One of her fact sheets shows that 25 gallons of water are needed to produce a pound of wheat, but 25,000 gallons are needed to produce a pound of meat. "The amount of water needed to produce one cow's worth of meat will float a large battleship," she says.

Many other issues concern her, not the least of which is meat's effect on oil supplies. "If a family of four," Yamunā says, "were to cut meat consumption two pounds a week, it would save 104 gallons of gasoline a year." And if America switched to a vegetarian diet, it would lower its imported oil requirement by 60%.

"For each person who kicks the meat habit, an acre of trees will be saved," she says.

"Here in Washington I meet lots of people striving to improve the quality of life. This has strengthened my view that we need to look at the big picture in considering vegetarianism. The diet I recommend is integrated with a holistic, spiritual worldview."

In other countries, such as Australia and the nations of Africa on the southern edge of the Sahara, cattle grazing and feed crop production on marginal lands contribute substantially to desertification.

Air Pollution

Burning of oil in the production of feed grain results in air pollution, including carbon dioxide, the main cause of global warming. Another major source of air pollution is the burning of tropical forests to clear land for cattle grazing.

The meat industry burns up a lot of fossil fuel, pouring pollutants into the air. Calorie for calorie, it takes 39 times more energy to produce beef than soybeans.[12] The petroleum used in the United States would decrease by 60% if people adopted a vegetarian diet.[13]

And in their book *For the Common Good*, World Bank economist Herman E. Daly and philosopher John B. Cobb, Jr. say, "If a simple and healthful change in eating habits along with localization of most food production and a major shift toward organic farming were to take place over the next generation, food production and distribution could be weaned from their current heavy dependence on fossil fuels. In the process, the enormous suffering now inflicted on livestock would be greatly reduced."[14]

The meat industry, in addition to producing carbon dioxide, is also responsible for other greenhouse gases, such as methane. Methane is produced directly by the digestive process of cows. This greenhouse gas is considered very dangerous because each molecule of methane traps 20 times more heat than a molecule of carbon dioxide.

How big a threat to the planet is the methane emitted by cows? Overall, the effect is not significant, certainly not enough to justify fears of cows destroying the planet by global warming. Each year about 500 million tons of methane enter the atmosphere,[15]contributing about 18% of the total greenhouse gases. Cows account for 60 million tons of the methane, about 12%.[16] Therefore, methane emitted by cows amounts to only 2% of the total greenhouse gas emissions. It should also be kept in mind that feedlot cows, because they eat more, produce more methane than range-fed cows. In India, there are about 270 million cows, but 99.9% of them are range fed.[17] They therefore produce less methane.

Water Pollution

About 50% of water pollution in the United States is linked to livestock.[18] Pesticides and fertilizers used in helping grow feed grains run off into lakes and rivers. They also pollute ground water. In the feedlots and stockyard holding pens, there is also a tremendous amount of pesticide runoff. Organic contaminants from huge concentrations of animal excrement and urine at feedlots and stockyards also pollute water. This waste is anywhere from ten to hundreds of times more concentrated than raw domestic sewage. According to a German documentary film (*Fleisch Frisst Menschen* [*Flesh Devours Man*] by Wolfgang Kharuna), nitrates evaporating from open tanks of concentrated livestock waste in the Netherlands have resulted in extremely high levels of forest-killing acid rain.

Water Depletion

All around the world, the beef industry is wasting the diminishing supplies of fresh water. For example, the livestock industry in the United States takes about 50% of the water consumed each year.[19]

Feeding the average meat eater requires about 4,200 gallons of water per day, versus 1,200 gallons per day for lacto-vegetarian diet.[20] While it takes only 25 gallons of water to produce a pound of wheat, it takes 2,500 gallons of water to produce a pound of meat.[21]

The Bottom Line

Reducing or eliminating meat consumption would have substantial positive effects on the environment. Fewer trees would be cut, less soil would be eroded, and desertification would be substantially slowed. A major source of air and water pollution would be removed, and scarce fresh water would be conserved. "To go beyond beef is to transform our very thinking about appropriate behavior toward nature," says Jeremy Rifkin. "We come to appreciate the source of our sustenance, the divinely inspired creation that deserves nurture and requires stewardship. Nature is no longer viewed as an enemy to be subdued and tamed."[22]

Other Reasons Not to Kill Cows

Of course, saving the environment is not the only reason it's good to avoid eating meat, particularly beef. These reasons, some of which we mentioned at the beginning of this chapter, are discussed at length in other books published by the Kṛṣṇa consciousness movement (see the resource section at the end of this book).

During the process of converting grain to meat, 90% of the protein, 99% of the carbohydrates, and 100% of the dietary fiber are lost.

It is well documented that vegetarians are less likely to contract certain kinds of heart disease and cancer. So better health is one of the benefits of the flesh-free, *karma*-free diet practiced by the Kṛṣṇa consciousness movement. This diet is not only healthier but also more satisfying to the mind and taste buds than meat-centered diets.

Furthermore, eliminating meat eating would release a vast quantity of food grain for human consumption, thus helping solve the problem of world hunger. And on an ethical level, stopping animal killing helps induce a greater respect for all kinds of life, including human.

Toward a Spiritual Solution

"In a fragile biosphere, the ultimate fate of humanity may depend on whether we can cultivate a deeper sense of self-restraint, founded on a widespread ethic of limiting consumption and finding non-material enrichment.[1]"

Alan Durning
World Watch Institute

H ow do people try to deal with the environmental crisis? Few are confronting the problem from the standpoint of spiritual consciousness.

Material Solutions (Individual)

Some are trying, however, to make changes in their normal daily activities, and this is good, especially in the industrial nations. The U.S., Europe, and Japan bear the most responsibility for the earth's environmental crisis. "The richest billion people in the world have created a form of civilization so acquisitive and profligate that the planet is in danger," says Alan Durning of the World Watch Institute. "The life-style of this top echelon—the car drivers, beef eaters, soda drinkers, and throwaway consumers—constitutes an ecological threat unmatched in severity."[2]

Concerned individuals manifest their personal commitment to a better environment by recycling paper and glass, by not purchasing products they consider harmful to the environment, and by giving money to support environmental action and awareness groups. They try to reduce their consumption of energy and the amount of water they use.

And in the Hare Kṛṣṇa movement, we also try to do some of those same things—not just because they are good for the environment but because they are good for our own spiritual development.

Our founding spiritual master, Śrīla A. C. Bhaktivedanta Swami Prabhupāda, was not only a great scholar of India's vast Vedic literature. He was also a reservoir of practical ecological wisdom, all based an the ancient spiritual culture of India. Right from his first years in the United States, in the 1960s, Śrīla Prabhupāda would do things that today would immediately be recognized as environmentally sound. Yet Śrīla Prabhupāda's attitudes and behavior, acquired during his years in India, initially astonished his disciples, who had been born into a consume-and-throw-away culture.

On the morning of May 31, 1976, Śrīla Prabhupāda was walking with some disciples on a beach in Honolulu, Hawaii. One of his disciples said, "People have exploited the atmosphere and the earth so badly in the last two hundred years especially that, practically speaking, man is on the verge of self-destruction." The disciple added that people were trying to solve the problem by, among other things, recycling.

But for Śrīla Prabhupāda, recycling was not something new. He explained how in India rural people take their broken metal utensils to merchants, who give them half the original price. Typically, even the bowls and plates Indian families use for dining are of metal, which can eventually be recycled.

On another occasion, in Rome, in May 1974, Śrīla Prabhupāda told his disciples how to save trees: "Paper you can make from grass, from cotton, from so many other fibers. You don't require wood. . . . From rejected paper, you can get another paper also. But they throw it away in your country. Collect this rejected paper and again put it into paper." This conversation took place years before recycling of paper became popular.

One might suspect that Śrīla Prabhupāda's thriftiness was only a habit from his life in India, in many respects a poor country. But there was more to it than that. Śrīla Prabhupāda saw the world and its resources as God's energy, and these were not to be misused and wasted, especially by people engaged in cultivating spiritual values.

Material Solutions (Collective)

Individual action is, of course, only part of the picture. People acting together, in groups large and small, are also grappling with the world's environmental problems.

For example, a group of parents, concerned about the health of their children, holds a demonstration to remove a toxic waste dump in the neighborhood. Some say this local grass roots approach is the most effective kind of an environmental action. In 1991, Hare Kṛṣṇa members in Poland led a successful grass roots movement to halt the opening of an environmentally harmful dolomite quarry. But for every grass roots group that succeeds, dozens of others fail to overcome the forces arrayed against them.

The bigger environmental action organizations, seeking more influence, stage national and even global events, such as Earth Day. They also lobby local, state, and national governments to adopt policies and regulations meant to broadly contribute to the solution of environmental problems. Many question the ultimate usefulness of this approach, which has been called "reform environmentalism." But it has had some positive effects.

The International Society for Krishna Consciousness has potential as a peaceful extragovernmental force for environmental change, nationally and internationally. In 1966, Śrīla Prabhupāda included in ISKCON's articles of incorporation a far-reaching statement of the movement's purposes. Among them: "To bring the members closer together for the purpose of teaching a simpler, more natural way of life."

Śrīla Prabhupāda did not, however, recommend high-pressure lobbying. Instead, he emphasized the establishment of self-sufficient agrarian communities. "If these farm projects

People Working for Change

Vanamālī Dāsa

In late 1990, four letters arrived on the desks of district authorities for the Polish village of Czarnow (pronounced Char-nov), population 70. One came from a leading member of parliament in Warsaw, the second from a Polish environmental inspector, the third from Poland's Minister of the Environment, and the fourth from the Minister of Minerals and Forests.

All indicated that a pending proposal to mine dolomite in Czarnow would violate existing laws. The letters warned local government leaders not to approve the mine project or a related proposal to lay an asphalt road through the village.

Two years after businessman Zenon Chwastek announced plans to build the dolomite mine in this peaceful hamlet, they were dead on the drawing board—due mainly to an unrelenting grass roots campaign led by Vanamālī Dāsa.

Born on August 25, 1963, in the Polish town of Siedlce, Vanamālī is chief priest of Czarnow's 220-acre Hare Kṛṣṇa community, New Shantipur (in Sanskrit "the New City of Peace"). A newcomer to Czarnow in 1985, Vanamālī made it one of his goals to live in a rural community free of industrial intrusion. Most of New Shantipur's land is tilled by teams of oxen, and the community is moving toward self-sufficiency, although it is still not yet growing all its own food. When he learned of the mine project in the summer of 1988, Vanamālī saw it as the death knell for the village. His determination to resist, he says, was born of his spiritual perspective, a vision of the village and its environs, which in his words constitute "a living organism whose psychological and ecological balance would have been destroyed by the mine operation."

Czarnow sits at 2,700 feet above sea level, 280 miles southwest of Warsaw, 60 miles from the Czech border. The picturesque village is a minor tourist attraction, appealing to those who like to stroll along its hilly pathways during the hot July-August season. At these times, about a hundred people a day, mostly those who put up at a local hostel, walk in small groups through winding lanes, shaded by hundreds of spruce, ash, and larch trees.

Part of Chwastek's mining proposal was that Czarnow's status as a conservation area be removed.

"It was an outrage," says Vanamālī. "The ecology of the region would have been damaged for the foreseeable future. Constant noise, carbon monoxide from the trucks, smoke, rock dust, petrol pumps, magazine and food stalls for truck drivers—where would it end? The village would have been permanently demoralized."

When he realized that Chwastek's plans were advancing unimpeded, Vanamālī began to visit the mayor, villagers, and residents in the neighboring localities. The quiet village gradually awoke to the threat, and Vanamālī soon collected 7,000 protest signatures from area residents.

He lobbied local officials and wrote relentlessly to key government figures in Warsaw.

Hundreds took part in a demonstration he led in Jelenia Gora on December 1, 1989, and the event received national media attention. Its protest banner "We Protest Building a Mine in Czarnow" dominated a front-page news photo in a local newspaper. Because of this effort, the village preserves its tranquil atmosphere.

are successful," he wrote to a disciple on September 29, 1975, "then all this industry will be closed. We do not have to make propaganda, but automatically people will not want it."

In recent years, some environmentalists have formed "green" political parties to win elections and carry out their programs from within governments, mainly in Europe.

In the middle 1970s, several members of the Hare Kṛṣṇa movement ran for city, state, and national offices in the United States. None were elected, but their campaigns did call attention to the theme of simple living in harmony with nature. It is possible that similar campaigns will be run in the future.

Most environmental problems, such as global warming, are so expansive that even national governments are not able to confront them alone. Coordinated efforts by many nations, indeed all nations, seem to be required.

The United Nations is, therefore, becoming more active in environmental issues and related causes such as sustainable economic growth. Some propose giving the Security Council a mandate to deal with environmental problems. Others have suggested the creation of a separate U.N. ecological council, with powers like those of the Security Council.[3]

Many assume that the magnitude of the world's environmental crisis will compel nations to cooperate. But Michael G. Renner of the World Watch Institute warns, "The world remains characterized by many conflicting interests and rivalries and plagued by enormous inequalities in power, wealth, and capacity to influence global affairs. Environmental concern could either provide the glue that helps humanity overcome these divisions or it could simply compound them."[4] One not so extreme possibility, symbolized by the burning of hundreds of oil wells in Kuwait during the Gulf War of 1990, is environmental warfare.

So despite collective efforts on all levels, the environmental crisis still deepens. The number of extinctions and endangered species increases. Rain forests and other kinds of forests continue to be lost. Large-scale mechanized agriculture, operating with chemical pesticides and fertilizers, degrades more and more of the earth's arable lands. Mountains of trash continue to pile up in the developed nations of the world, as recycling efforts fail, partly because of lack of a market for recycled materials. No really safe long-range solutions for the disposal of toxic and nuclear waste have yet been found. Despite decades of government regulation, levels of water pollution and air pollution remain intolerably high.

Further, the problems of global warming and ozone depletion have compelled nations to conclude that drastic measures are required. But governments appear to lack the will to institute such measures. For example, in 1992 heads of the world's nations met in Rio de Janeiro at an environmental summit meeting. They watered down the centerpiece of the conference, a treaty on global warming. They also eliminated provisions for mandatory definite reductions in carbon dioxide emissions.

Most collective attempts to cope with pollution rely on end-of-the-pipeline control and treatment rather than prevention. This approach has not, however, succeeded. A way has to be found, it seems, to stop the pollution at its source, but this has proved almost impossible.

The Myth of Overpopulation

Those who buy into the concept of overpopulation claim that the very number of people living on the planet is one of the major threats to the environment. Therefore, they say, government-sponsored population control programs, especially abortion, are essential.

But the very word "overpopulation" is loaded with questionable assumptions and negative value judgments about the number of people living on this planet and the earth's capacity to sustain them.

The nature and effects of so-called overpopulation are

generally misrepresented. Over the past few decades, we have heard many predictions of massive famines, but these have failed to materialize. This is not to say that there is not a problem of hunger in the world. But this hunger is caused more by abnormally low rainfall, political unrest, and economic exploitation than by "overpopulation."

In terms of living space, the world as a whole is far from being crowded. A simple calculation shows that every man, woman, and child (about 6 billion total) could be placed within the 210,038 square miles of France, with each person having about 975 square feet of space.

But what about food? A study by the University of California's Division of Agricultural Science shows that by practicing the best agricultural methods now in use, the world's farmers could raise enough food to provide a meat-centered diet for a population 10 times greater than at present. But that's not the limit. If people would be satisfied with an equally nourishing but mostly vegetarian diet, a population 30 times greater than at present could be fed, the study shows. A switch to a vegetarian diet would also bring many environmental improvements—less destruction of rain forests, less air pollution, and less water pollution, to name a few.

In the early 1970s there was some famine in sub-Saharan Africa, but studies have shown that every country affected also had, within its own borders, sufficient agricultural resources to feed its own people. As Frances Moore Lappé points out in her well-researched book *Food First*, much of the best land was being misused for production of cash export crops. And this is still true today, not only in the sub-Sahara but throughout the world.

The same phenomenon was noted by Śrīla Prabhupāda, the founder of the Kṛṣṇa consciousness movement. During a visit to Mauritius in 1975, he stated in a lecture attended by some of the nation's leading citizens: "So I see in your Mauritius island you have got enough land to produce food grains." He then challenged, "I understand that instead of growing food grains you are growing sugar cane for exporting. Why? . . . You first of all grow your own eatables, and if there is time and if your population has sufficient food grains, then you can try to grow other fruits and vegetables for exporting."

He went on to say, "I have traveled to Africa, Australia, and America, and everywhere there is so much land vacant that if we use it to produce food grains then we can feed 10 times as much population as at the present moment. There is no question of scarcity. The whole creation is so made by Kṛṣṇa that everything is *pūrṇam,* complete."

Another wasteful use of food resources has to do with diet. Śrīla Prabhupāda said during his lecture in Mauritius: "I have seen in the Western countries they are growing food grains for the animals, and the food grains are eaten by the animals, and the animal is eaten by the man . . . what are the statistics? The animals are eating food grains, but the same amount of food grains can be eaten by so many men."

Such statistics do exist. About 90% of the edible grains harvested in the U.S. is fed to animals that are later killed for meat production. But for every 16 pounds of grain fed to beef cattle, only 1 pound of meat is obtained in return. The same wasteful use of grain to fatten feedlot cattle for meat is commonplace in Western Europe, Australia, New Zealand, and Japan.

Śrīla Prabhupāda concluded, "If there were one government on the surface of the earth to handle the distribution of grain, there would be no question of scarcity, no necessity to open slaughterhouses, and no need to present false theories about overpopulation."[5]

The first person to sound the overpopulation alarm was the English economist Thomas Robert Malthus (1766–1834), who calculated that the world's population tends to increase faster than its food supply. Interestingly enough, Malthus

People Working for Change

Ian Roberts

"In June 1992 I had the good fortune to attend the Earth Summit in Rio de Janeiro," says Ian Roberts, Director of Leicester Environment City. "The conference was designed to allow world leaders to debate the problems of environmental degradation and economic disorder. The issues appeared alarmingly complex. Government leaders from around the world could not devise specific and meaningful solutions. As I thought through the issues on the Earth Summit agenda, I reflected on a statement in the *Bhagavad-gītā As It Is* which tells us that by contemplating the objects of the senses one becomes attached to them and ultimately frustrated and bewildered. Industrialized society in particular has as its cornerstone the need to stimulate consumption, to constantly fuel economic growth. To this end it constantly encourages us to meditate on the objects of our senses. With individuals' desires massively outstripping their abilities to meet their aspirations, is it any surprise that we create ongoing frustration and extreme egotism, which result in environmental, social, and cultural devastation? The *Gītā* offers a simple solution to these anomalies, linking our problems directly to our lack of spiritual culture and value."

Ian grew up in the British Midlands and studied civil engineering at Liverpool University. In 1980, he graduated and went to work for British Petroleum.

"Throughout the '80s I worked in areas of extraordinary natural beauty, in Africa, Australia, and New Zealand," says Ian. "Watching the degradation of these areas made me realize that we must identify means of meeting people's needs today without jeopardizing the needs of their future."

One day a newspaper article caught Ian's eye. The city of Leicester, England, was looking for a director to manage a new project designed to turn the city into a model of "green" development.

The goal would be to green Leicester, Britain's tenth largest city, within four years. Ian applied for the job and got it.

The project developed rapidly. At the United Nations Earth Summit, Leicester's Environment City project was selected as one of the world's top twelve environmental projects.

The Environment City partnership has improved bicycle paths and recycling facilities. It has also brought environmental education to schools with its "Faith in Nature" program, involving all of Leicester's faith groups.

Ian is convinced that sustainable improvements in the environment will occur only with changes in people's values and beliefs. "The policies devised and implemented under the Environment City banner in Leicester have had a common theme," he says, "to encourage individuals to reduce the consumption of nature's limited resources. At the same time we have to show that the quality of life can be improved when material consumption is decreased." Without this change in emphasis, the changes that are desperately required will not take place.

"It is clear to all thinking people that radical and lasting change in our society is necessary. Such change is technically and economically feasible and socially desirable. So what is lacking? I would say we are desperately short of leadership and spiritual guidance. Our environmental crisis is a crisis of the human spirit."

believed that the best solution was voluntary restraint in sex.

Toward a Spiritual Solution

Everyone seems to agree that we have to cut down the amount of damage we're doing to the environment. But this brings us to a real crunch. We run up against the individual desire for accumulating wealth through manufacturing, mechanized agriculture, trade, banking, and finance. We run up against the conviction that a nation's strength is measured by the growth of its industrial capacity. We run up against the consumer mentality, which identifies happiness with the ability to acquire, through high-paying jobs, more and more material possessions. It's an impossible situation—we want a clean, healthy environment, yet at the same time too many of us demand a style and standard of life that inevitably results in environmental degradation.

A number of thoughtful people have, however, recognized this dilemma and proposed solutions requiring fundamental changes in human consciousness, in the direction of simpler living and the pursuit of nonmaterial satisfaction.

For the members of the Hare Kṛṣṇa movement, including ourselves, such ideas are not new. Śrīla Prabhupāda, the movement's founder, once said, "Life is never made comfortable by artificial needs but by plain living and high thinking."[6] We find it encouraging that others are coming to the conclusion that human energy has to somehow be "dovetailed to the complete whole." Although we may not agree with everyone on every point, we are hopeful that by a combined effort we can make progress toward a real solution to our planet's environmental crisis.

Deep Ecology

One group that sees the need for a fundamental change in human consciousness is the "deep ecologists." A good overview of deep ecology theory can be found in *Deep Ecology*, by environmentalist Bill Devall and philosopher George Sessions. "Deep ecology is a process of ever-deeper questioning of ourselves, the assumptions of the dominant worldview in our culture, and the meaning and truth of our reality," say Devall and Sessions.[7]

The International Society for Krishna Consciousness is, we feel safe in saying, an organization that addresses the deep philosophical and spiritual issues that touch on the self and nature, while simultaneously introducing a way of life that situates the self harmoniously within nature. We sense the beginning of a cultural migration in the world—a deliberate movement, not primarily from one place to another, although that may be part of it, but from one state of mind to another. And we see ourselves as part of that shift in values and involved in creating the alternative social structures to support it.

We agree with the deep ecologists that modern civilization raises obstacles to the attainment of this shift in values. "In technocratic industrial societies there is overwhelming propaganda and advertising which encourages false needs and destructive desires designed to foster increased production and consumption of goods," say Devall and Sessions. "Most of this actually diverts us from facing reality in an objective way and from beginning the 'real work' of spiritual growth and maturity."[8]

Deep ecologists would like to see much of the world returned to wilderness conditions. They also speak of the "biocentric equality" of all living things. By this they mean that "all things in the biosphere have an equal right to live and blossom and to reach their own individual forms of unfolding and self-realization within the larger Self-realization."[9]

This attitude echoes the timeless vision of the ancient Vedic sages of India, whose teachings the members of the modern Kṛṣṇa consciousness movement follow. "The humble sage, by virtue of true knowledge, sees with equal vision a learned and gentle *brāhmaṇa,* a cow, an elephant, a dog, and a dog-eater [outcaste]," says the *Bhagavad-gītā* (5.18).

"A Kṛṣṇa conscious person does not make any distinction between species or castes," comments Śrīla Prabhupāda on this text in his *Bhagavad-gītā As It Is.* "The *brāhmaṇa* and the outcaste may be different from the social point of view, or a dog, a cow, and an elephant may be different from the species point of view, but these differences are meaningless from the viewpoint of a learned transcendentalist. This is due to their relationship to the Supreme."

Voluntary Simplicity and Nonmaterial Satisfaction

The call for spiritual change as a solution to the world's environmental problems sometimes comes from unexpected places. At first glance, the World Watch Institute, based in Washington, D.C., looks like just one more organization turning out well-documented reports on the world's environmental problems. The Institute's yearly *State of the World* report has become a standard reference for government officials, educators, and journalists around the world.

But the World Watch Institute goes beyond identifying problems and proposing end-of-the-pipeline solutions. It also makes proposals for spiritually oriented solutions.

In a recent *State of the World* report, Institute director Lester Brown and his associates Christopher Flavin and Sandra Postel asserted, "Throughout the ages, philosophers and religious leaders have denounced materialism as a viable path to human fulfillment. Yet societies across the ideological spectrum have persisted in equating quality of life with increased consumption. . . . Because of the strain on resources it creates, materialism simply cannot survive the transition to a sustainable world."[10]

Alan Durning, a senior researcher of the World Watch Institute, says, "In a fragile biosphere, the ultimate fate of humanity may depend on whether we can cultivate a deeper sense of self-restraint, founded on a widespread ethic of limiting consumption and finding nonmaterial enrichment."[11]

In considering how to accomplish this transformation of consciousness, Durning finds value in "the body of human wisdom passed down from antiquity." He urges environmentally concerned people "to follow the path of voluntary simplicity preached by all sages from Buddha to Mohammed."

Voluntary simplicity is, however, a difficult goal to achieve. "It would be hopelessly naive to believe that entire populations will suddenly experience a moral awakening, renouncing greed, envy, and avarice," says Durning.[12] But some people, including members of the International Society for Krishna Consciousness, are moving in that direction.

At present, more than 40 of our 360 worldwide centers are rural, and they are moving, some more rapidly than others, toward self-sufficiency. Even the urban centers of the Krsna consciousness movement teach the spiritual philosophy of simple living and high thinking. They also direct attention to the rural settlements that are helping establish an appropriate direction for the future of the planet.

We certainly don't claim to have articulated or implemented complete solutions. But perhaps we can help widen the circle of those who see the problem as a spiritual one. Such people see the entire world and all her creatures as part of a unified whole. Experiencing satisfaction from within, they are becoming liberated from the excessive greed that drives the world toward environmental destruction. The simpler, more natural way of life they follow contributes to a cleaner, more peaceful and beautiful world.

4
Science, Nature, and the Environment

"The desacralized world is doomed to become an obstacle inviting conquest, a mere object. Like the animal or the slave who is understood to have no soul, it becomes a thing of subhuman status to be worked, used up, and exploited."[1]

Theodore Roszak
Where the Wasteland Ends

Among those calling for a spiritual solution to our planet's environmental crisis are, interestingly enough, some of the world's leading scientists. At the Global Forum of Spiritual and Parliamentary Leaders, held in Moscow in January 1990, 32 scientists signed a document titled "Preserving and Cherishing the Earth: An Appeal for Joint Commitment in Science and Religion."

The signers included astronomer Carl Sagan, nuclear winter theorist Paul J. Crutzen, physicist Freeman J. Dyson, paleontologist Stephen J. Gould, environmental scientist Roger Revelle, and former Massachusetts Institute of Technology (MIT) president Jerome Wiesner.

The scientists said, "We are close to committing—many would argue we are already committing—what in religious language is sometimes called Crimes against Creation," said the scientists. They therefore issued an urgent "appeal to the world religious community to commit, in word and deed, and as boldly as is required, to preserve the environment of the earth."

"The environmental crisis requires radical changes not only in public policy," said the scientists, "but also in individual behavior. The historical record makes clear that religious teaching, example, and leadership are powerfully able to influence personal conduct and commitment."

"As scientists, many of us have had profound experiences of awe and reverence before the universe," added the signers. "We understand that what is regarded as sacred is more likely to be treated with care and respect. Our planetary home should be so regarded. Efforts to safeguard and cherish the environment need to be infused with a vision of the sacred."

Ironically, science more than anything else has been responsible for the destruction of "the vision of the sacred." Although the signers speak carefully of crimes against "Creation," scientists such as signer Stephen J. Gould are unremittingly hostile to any hint of "Creation" in science classrooms. Although such scientists may see in religion a force for social change, they deny that religion has anything significant to say about the origin of life and the universe. Religion, according to many prominent scientists, is nothing more than a pattern of behavior that arose in the mind of evolving humans. Because it gave some groups of humans an advantage in the struggle for survival, religion—scientists say—has persisted. And it is to this social utility of religion that the signers of the Moscow document opportunistically appealed.

Religionists could best respond to the scientists who signed the Moscow document by reclaiming the world from blind materialism and channeling human energy into spiritual development. This would mean confronting both the worldview of modern science and the urban-industrial civilization it has spawned. Unfortunately, most religious leaders appear unwilling to take these steps.

The Roots of the Environmental Crisis In the Scientific Revolution

Our environmental problems are a natural and predictable by-product of the science-based, technocratic civilization that originated a few centuries ago in Europe and spread around the world.

In preindustrial Europe of the Middle Ages, people assumed that human life had a divine purpose and destination. As such, material progress played a role in society subordinate to that of spiritual elevation.

Robert S. Lopez, a professor of history at Yale University in the United States, said of the medieval thinkers: "They did not need to grope, like Einstein, for a unified theory of physics. God, they felt, provided that unity. He was the order of the world, the harmonizer of all contrasts, the initiator of all motions. Love gushing from Him to all creatures and returned to Him by the creatures in proportion to their abilities was (as one would say today) the source of all energies."[2]

Indian civilization shared this vision. The five-thousand-year-old *Śrīmad-Bhāgavatam* (1.2.6) contains this message about the ultimate purpose of human life: "The supreme occupation [*dharma*] for all humanity is that by which men can attain to loving devotional service unto the transcendent Lord."

Even as Europe entered the age of scientific discovery, many of the early scientists retained deep and profound conceptions of God as the ultimate controller and designer of the universe. Copernicus (1473–1543) is idolized by modern intellectuals for his assertion that the sun occupies the central place in the solar system, a view orthodox Churchmen of the time rejected. Yet even as he calculated the vast distances of stars and planets, Copernicus wrote that their orbits were an illustration of the "divine work of the Great and Noble Creator."

But as the growth of science in the Renaissance and Enlightenment eras in Europe continued, the outlines of the hand of God grew dimmer and dimmer on the canvas of the universe. The universe became a colder, more impersonal place, governed not by divine arrangement and intercession but by precise, mathematically expressed physical laws. Thus began a philosophy that still lies at the heart of science. It is called reductionism—the attempt to reduce the universe, including all human experience, to measurable and predictable states of

People Working for Change

Brahmapāda Dāsa

Brahmapāda Dāsa's day begins at 4:15 a.m. when he walks half a mile through the darkness, along a meter-wide dirt path flanked by banana trees and rice fields, to a large, brightly lit Vedic temple. Here he joins others in singing prayers before life-size Deities of Rādhā and Kṛṣṇa during a morning service, known as *mangal arotika* ("auspicious time for worship").

By 5:30 a.m. he has returned to his residence, a simple structure situated 10 yards from the sheds that house 80 cows, bulls, calves, and bullocks. The sheds are known as the "Māyāpur Dairy Farm" or, in local parlance, the *goshala,* "shelter for cows." By 6:00 a.m. Brahmapāda begins to supervise 14 workers who wash, feed, and milk the animals, turning them out to pasture by 9:00.

Māyāpur is a 700-acre Hare Kṛṣṇa community situated on the river Ganges in West Bengal, India, 30 miles from the Bangladesh border. Two hundred forty residents live at Māyāpur, and its organizers are developing it as a planned town for 25,000 residents, based on Vedic models of community and village life.

Brahmapāda was born in 1955, in Masibad district (near Barhampur), 66 miles from Māyāpur. He joined the Māyāpur community in 1976 when he was 21 years old, 6 years after meeting Māyāpur residents. They had traveled through his small village in a traditional *nagar kīrtana* party, singing the names of Kṛṣṇa.

Shortly after joining the Māyāpur community, Brahmapāda began to work in the *goshala*, tending what was then a small herd of about 30 cows. He did everything himself—pumped water, cut cow fodder, fed the animals, put them out to pasture, milked them, and tilled fodder fields with ox-driven plows. Having grown up on a farm, this work came naturally to him. "I felt content doing this work, but I was especially satisfied knowing that I was farming for Kṛṣṇa," he says.

In 1977, he was given personal spiritual initiation by the founder of the Hare Kṛṣṇa movement, His Divine Grace A.C. Bhaktivedanta Swami Prabhupāda, who had also been born in Bengal. Brahmapāda made up his mind to work in the Māyāpur dairy farm for the rest of his life.

He takes special pride in the *goshala's* 3 biogas (*gobar*) generators. These supply gas that cooks meals for 110 people 3 times a day.

"The government people came in jeeps and asked us to make these generators," he says. "They offered to pay half the expenses. It's difficult to get electricity out here for cooking, and there's not much wood to make cooking fires."

Through an opening near the top of each tank, workers introduce a mixture of 3 parts cow dung to 5 parts water. This preparation ferments, producing a natural gas. As it expands, gas rises to the top of the tank and is pressured into a pipe leading from the top. The pipes from all 3 *gobar* tanks then join to become one pipe that leads into the kitchen, where it splits into 4 to power the gas burners on which the meals are cooked. The slurry remaining in the tanks makes an excellent agricultural fertilizer.

Brahmapāda also plans to use biogas to light rooms in some of the *goshala* buildings in which devotees live and to construct more generating tanks for cooking, light, and heat. "After the passage of years, we will see that these tanks have saved us a lot of money, wood, labor, and time," he says.

actions of matter (ultimately subatomic particles) and material forces (such as electromagnetism and gravity).

But the new scientists were not simply interested in knowledge for knowledge's sake. Sir Francis Bacon (1561–1626), one of the main founders of the modern scientific method, said that "knowledge is power," a lesson the atomic scientists of the twentieth century were to learn only too well. In her book *The Death of Nature,* historian Carolyn Merchant points out that Bacon felt nature had to be "hounded in her wanderings" and "made a slave."[3] The business of the scientist was "to torture nature's secrets from her."

In the seventeenth century, Bacon listed in *The New Atlantis* some of the inventions he could foresee, "The prolongation of life . . . means to convey sound in trunks and pipes in strange lines and distances . . . flying in the air . . . ships and boats for going under water." Also in the list: "instruments of destruction as of war and poison" and "engines of war, stronger and more violent, exceeding our greatest cannons."[4]

Religion began to lose its importance with the rise of science and technology. Social critic and historian Lewis Mumford said, "Whatever their adhesion to the outward ceremonies of the Church . . . more and more people began to act as if their happiness, their prosperity, their salvation were to be achieved on the earth alone, by means they themselves would if possible command."[5]

In the eighteenth and nineteenth centuries, as the view of the world became even more materialistic, greater human effort was channeled into building the machines Bacon envisioned, vastly increasing human ability to exploit the earth's resources. Thus began the industrial revolution, which generated the environmental crises we now confront.

One of the first industries to expand was mining, which initially met with considerable opposition. Medieval European philosophers, following their Greek and Roman predecessors, claimed it was morally wrong to mine metals from the earth.

Pliny (A.D. 23–79), for example, wrote in his *Natural History* that the earth, "bounteous and ever ready," supplies us from her surface "with all things for our benefit." But the substances below the surface "urge us to our ruin" while "exhausting the earth."[6]

The medieval opponents of large-scale mining had a surprisingly prophetic view of its negative environmental effects. In 1556, Georg Agricola wrote in *De Re Metallica*: "The strongest argument of the detractors [of mining] is that the fields are devastated by mining operations. . . . Also they argue that the woods and groves are cut down, for there is need of wood for timbers, machines, and the smelting of metals. And when the woods and groves are felled, then are exterminated the beasts and birds. . . . Further, when the ores are washed, the water which has been used poisons the brooks and streams, and either destroys the fish or drives them away."

In the village communities of many areas of medieval Europe, land was held and used in ways that were not very destructive to the environment. Pastures, forests, and water resources were held in common, and their use was carefully regulated by councils of village officials or elders.

The agricultural system was directed toward local self-sufficiency. With the decline of the medieval God-centered world view and the rise of materialistic science and industry, this subsistence type of agriculture dwindled. Between the years 1500 and 1700, it was gradually replaced by production for the emerging market economy. The application of industrial methods of production to agriculture set in motion a process that is even now destroying traditional village economies and the environment.

The combined impact of market agriculture and expanding industry began the rapid depletion of Europe's forests in the sixteenth century. Trees were cut to expand farmland and pasture and to supply fuel and raw materials for factories. During the seventeeth century, England, now faced with a shortage of wood, switched to coal as an energy source for industry. "Whereas the medieval economy had been based on organic and renewable energy sources—wood, water, and wind—the emerging capitalist economy taking shape over most of western Europe was based not only on the nonrenewable energy source—coal—but on an inorganic economic core—metals: iron, copper, silver, gold, tin, and mercury—the refining and processing of which ultimately depended on and further depleted the forests," says Carolyn Merchant.[7]

The soft coal used as fuel in England had a high sulfur content and produced thick, black, choking smoke. In 1627, a petition complained that coal smoke was tainting pastures and poisoning fish in the Thames.[8]

Worldview and Culture

The pattern that emerged in medieval and Renaissance Europe—a progressively more godless cosmology leading to a destructive civilization based on the maximum exploitation of matter—was described five thousand years ago in the *Bhagavad-gītā*.

The *Gītā* (16.4, 7–16) states: "They say that this world is unreal, with no foundation, no God in control. . . . Following such conclusions, the demoniac, who are lost to themselves and who have no intelligence, engage in unbeneficial, horrible acts meant to destroy the world. . . . They believe that to gratify the senses is the prime necessity of human civilization."

Some modern observers echo the *Gītā's* words. Pitirim Sorokin, former chairman of Harvard University's department of sociology, described the civilization that rose out of Renaissance Europe's age of scientific discovery as "sensate." Sensate culture, he explained, "is based upon the ultimate principle that . . . beyond the reality and values which we can see, hear, smell, touch, and taste there is no other reality and no real values."[9]

Sorokin said that sensate society "Intensely cultivates scientific knowledge of the physical and biological properties of sensory reality."[10] He adds, "Despite its lip service to the values of the Kingdom of God, it cares mainly about the sensory values of wealth, health, bodily comfort, sensual pleasures, and lust for power and fame. Its dominant ethic is invariably utilitarian and hedonistic." The inevitable result, Sorokin said, is the exceptional violence we have experienced in the twentieth century. And we may include in this category violence against the planet itself, brought on by the "increasing destructiveness of the morally irresponsible, sensate scientific achievements . . . invented and continuously perfected by the sensate scientists."[11]

5
A Science of Consciousness

"As the sun alone illuminates all this universe, so does the living entity, one within the body, illuminate the entire body by consciousness."

Bhagavad-gītā 13.34

I f the world is to ever become free from the threat of environmental annihilation, we shall have to undertake a thorough reexamination of the materialistic assumptions underlying not only our picture of nature but our conception of our very selves.

Some scientists are already beginning to question whether materialistic principles are really adequate to explain basic features of human existence—such as consciousness. For example, John C. Eccles, a Nobel-prize-winning neurobiologist, states, "The ultimate problem relates to the origin of the self, how each of us as a self-conscious being comes to exist as a unique self associated with a brain. This is the mystery of personal existence." Eccles said that "the uniqueness each of us experiences can be sufficiently explained only by recourse to some supernatural origin."[1]

If the conscious self is factually supernatural in origin, and if this knowledge were firmly integrated into our educational and cultural institutions, society would probably be much more directed toward self-realization than it is today. The overwhelming impetus toward the domination and exploitation of matter that underlies today's industrial civilization and culminates in environmental catastrophe would certainly be lessened.

Insights from the Bhagavad-gītā

According to the *Bhagavad-gītā,* our unique sense of

individual experience results from the presence within the material body of a spiritual particle, the symptom of which is consciousness. "As the sun alone illuminates all this universe," states the *Gītā* (13.34), "so does the living entity, one within the body, illuminate the entire body by consciousness." Śrīla Prabhupāda comments, "Thus consciousness is the proof of the presence of the soul, as sunshine or light is the proof of the presence of the sun. When the soul is present in the body, there is consciousness all over the body, and as soon as the soul has passed from the body there is no more consciousness. This can be easily understood by any intelligent man. Therefore consciousness is not a product of the combinations of matter. It is the symptom of the living entity."

The nonmaterial nature of consciousness was understood by the famous nineteenth-century British scientist Thomas Huxley, who stated, "I understand the main tenet of materialism to be that there is nothing in the universe but matter and force; and that all the phenomena of nature are explicable by deduction from the properties assignable to these two primitive factors. . . . It seems to me pretty plain that there is a third thing in the universe, to wit, consciousness, which . . . I cannot see to be matter or force, or any conceivable modification of either."[2]

The *Gītā* (2.20, 2.17) offers extensive information about the nature of the nonmaterial particle that imparts the symptoms of life to the material body: "For the soul there is neither birth nor death at any time. He has not come into being, does not come into being, and will not come into being. He is unborn, eternal, ever-existing, and primeval. He is not slain when the body is slain. . . . That which pervades the entire body you should know to be indestructible. No one is able to destroy that imperishable soul."

The Sanskrit word often used for soul is *ātmā,* which means "the self." The *Gītā* (2.23–24) gives these further characteristics of the *ātmā:* "The soul can never be cut to pieces by any weapon, nor burned by fire, nor moistened by water, nor withered by the wind. The individual soul is unbreakable and insoluble, and can be neither burned nor dried. He is everlasting, present everywhere, unchangeable, immovable, and eternally the same."

Śrīla Prabhupāda comments, "The individual particle of spirit soul is a spiritual atom smaller than the material atoms, and such atoms are innumerable. This very small spiritual spark is the basic principle of the material body, and the influence of such a spiritual spark is spread all over the body as the influence of the active principle of some medicine spreads throughout the body. This current of the spirit soul is felt all over the body as consciousness, and that is the proof of the presence of the soul. Any layman can understand that the material body minus consciousness is a dead body, and this consciousness cannot be revived in the body by any means of material administration. Therefore, consciousness is not due to any amount of material combination, but to the spirit soul."

Empirical Evidence for the Ātmā

Although this line of thought may appear logical, one might still ask if there is any scientific evidence for the existence of the soul. Of course, if there actually is a nonmaterial entity one would not expect that it would be easily detectable by material instruments and empirical methods. Yet some fields of scientific research do give evidence for a conscious self that can exist apart from the physical mechanism of the body.

The medical field provides substantial data on out-of-body or near-death experiences (NDEs). Not uncommonly, patients subjected to extreme trauma, during accidents or sudden attacks of illness or operations, experience their conscious selves separating from their bodies. For example, people who have been treated for heart attacks report seeing their own bodies from a point above the operating table. But according to current medical understanding these patients should have

People Working for Change

Gokula Dāsa

In the early 1980s, Greg was working as a supervising draftsman for Telecom, Australia's national telecommunications company.

"My secret ambition was always to live in a mud brick house and to become self-sufficient on a small plot of land," says Gokula Dāsa (formerly Greg Brown), reflecting back on a time before he had committed himself to the life of Krṣṇa consciousness.

In 1987, he fulfilled his desire to live on a farm committed to developing long-term self-sufficiency. The recently purchased 250-acre property, 75 miles south of Melbourne, was named New Nandagram, after a village in India near the holy city of Vrṇdāvana, where Krṣṇa Himself lived about 5,000 years ago.

Gokula became one of the settlement's most inspired workers. His enthusiasm and flair for organization soon earned him a prominent position in the community. In 1991, he became farm manager of New Nandagram.

He contacted a mud-brick maker named Darius Bartlett, who donated machinery and time, teaching Gokula how to make bricks for a *brahmacārī āśrama* (dormitory for celibate men). Bartlett suggested that Gokula contact Peter Lockyer, a permaculture architect specializing in mud-brick construction. He did this, and eventually Peter introduced him to David Holmgren, a nearby resident and coauthor with Bill Mollisen of the book

Permaculture, which means "permanent agriculture." Gokula had learned about the permaculture concept years earlier and had hoped to make personal use of it someday. In July of 1992, he became a qualified permaculture design consultant.

"We decided to create a 20-year master plan for New Nandagram with David Holmgren. It took nearly a year to complete, but it was well worth the time and effort we put into it," says Gokula.

"We're planting 40,000 trees and shrubs," says Gokula. "A certain percentage of these will be fodder trees for the cows. They will supply additional feed when pasture growth is slow, as well as shelter from the extremes of heat and cold." The added shelter from the trees, he explains, also reduces stress on the cows, and this increases milk production. Fodder trees eliminate tractor and fuel costs and cut back on labor needed for the cutting, raking, baling, storing, and feeding of hay to the cows when pasture is scarce.

"We're using many common-sense methods employed by people living for centuries before the industrial revolution. New and old forests will save topsoil during the rains and provide firewood, building timbers, posts for fencing, wood for furniture, honey, and mulch for the crops and gardens.

"We'll produce dairy products and use ox power as our primary energy and transportation resource. We're learning exactly how to measure and maximize milk production and to control breeding so that the number of cows and bulls stays at equilibrium. In fact, this formula, and appropriate variations of it according to climate and other circumstances, I think may soon become the basis of cow protection on many other Hare Kṛṣṇa farms throughout the world, even in India.

"I want New Nandagram to become a window for Australians to see how we've incorporated the permaculture concept into a sustainable system based on cow protection and lacto-vegetarianism. It's permaculture adapted to the village life and culture of Vedic India."

been completely unconscious.

Although some reports of NDEs are questionable, reputable scientists have made convincing studies. Among these highly qualified researchers is Dr. Michael Sabom, a cardiologist and professor at the Emory University Medical School in Atlanta, Georgia (USA). Initially skeptical of the NDEs, Sabom changed his mind after conducting a thorough investigation.

In his book *Recollections of Death: A Medical Investigation,* Sabom gives dozens of documented accounts of near-death experiences. For example, one man said, "I was walking across the parking lot to get into my car . . . I passed out. I don't recall hitting the ground. The next thing I do recall was that I was above the cars, floating. I had a real funny sensation, a floating sensation. I was actually looking down on my own body, with four or five men running toward me. I could hear and understand what these men were saying."[3]

But the core of Sabom's book was a detailed study of heart attack patients. Sabom divided them into two groups. The first group, consisting of 25 patients, did not report any near-death experiences. When he asked them to give details about their heart attack treatment in the hospital, none gave a correct description.

The second group consisted of 32 patients who had reported near-death experiences during their heart attacks. When asked to describe their treatment, six gave descriptions that corresponded in detail to their medical records, although they should have been unconscious at the time. This result supported the view that these patients had in fact been looking at their bodies, and the treatment they were being given, from a point outside their bodies.

Sabom stated, "If the human brain is actually composed of two fundamental elements—the 'mind' and the 'brain'—then could the near-death crisis event somehow trigger a transient splitting of the mind from the brain in many individuals? . . .

My own beliefs on this matter are leaning in this direction. The out-of-body hypothesis simply seems to fit best with the data at hand. . . . Could the mind which splits apart from the physical brain be, in essence, the soul, which continues to exist after final bodily death, according to some religious doctrines? As I see it, this is the ultimate question that has been raised by reports of the NDE."[4]

There's a second category of scientific evidence suggesting that the self is a conscious entity that can exist apart from the physical body. These are reports of past lives memories. Here again is a field in which there is understandably much room for skepticism. Nevertheless, serious researchers have carried out painstaking investigations. Among them is Ian Stevenson, Carlson Professor of Psychiatry at the University of Virginia (USA). Stevenson has performed in-depth studies of reincarnation memories, focusing exclusively on memories reported by children, who are less likely than adults to have the motive or resources to fabricate recollections of past lives. In many cases Stevenson was able to verify extensive details of the accounts given by the children, confirming the existence of the places and persons described by them, including the dead person that they claimed to have been in their previous life.[5]

As of 1983, Stevenson had recorded about 2,500 reports of reincarnation memories. Of these, he said 881 had been investigated, and in 546 cases he and his team of researchers had verified details of the previous life reported by the subject. In other words, out of the total number of investigated cases, 62 per cent had resulted in this kind of confirmation of the reported past life. Many of these cases are reported in Stevenson's four-volume compendium titled *Cases of the Reincarnation Type,* published by the University Press of Virginia.

Dr. Peter Ramster, a psychologist at the University of Sydney, Australia, has performed similar research involving adults who reported past lives memories under hypnosis. Accompanied by independent observers, he took some of these subjects to the places of their reported past lives, where he verified even the minutest details of their memories.

In addition to past life memories, both Ramster and Stevenson present evidence of xenoglossy (unexpected knowledge of foreign languages) under hypnosis. Stevenson reports a case of an American housewife who fluently spoke an old Swedish dialect under hypnosis, although she had no known exposure to Swedish throughout her life.[6] Such reports of xenoglossy indicate that the conscious self within a given physical body may have existed previously in a different physical body and was able to carry with it knowledge from that previous existence.

But today, influenced by materialistic science's refusal to consider the existence of a nonmaterial conscious self, people tend to identify exclusively with the body and mind. They therefore tend to exploit matter for the purpose of continually increasing their bodily satisfaction. Expressed through today's urban-industrial civilization, this exploitation is causing environmental decay of unprecedented global proportions.

The *Bhagavad-gītā* and other works of Vedic literature provide a theoretical understanding that the self is different from the body. But for realizing this there are practical programs of yoga and meditation—such as the chanting of the Hare Kṛṣṇa *mantra*. This gives direct perception of the self. In *The Science of Self-Realization,* Śrīla Prabhupāda says, "If one chants the Hare Kṛṣṇa *mantra*, he will realize that he is not this material body. 'I do not belong to this material body or this material world. I am a spirit soul, part and parcel of the Supreme.'"[7]

Understanding the difference between our temporary material identity and our true spiritual identity is the key to solving the environmental crisis. The foundation for an environmentally healthy planet is a science of consciousness that incorporates knowledge of the soul.

Karma and the Environment

"Quite apart from the laws of physics and chemistry, as laid down in quantum theory, we must consider laws of quite a different kind."[1]

Niels Bohr
Nobel laureate in physics

Many see the environmental problem as strictly technical, with technical solutions. Even those who see an ethical dimension may see solutions only in terms of mobilizing public opinion to change certain obvious environmentally destructive behaviors. But there are deeper dimensions to the environmental crisis.

In addition to the laws presently known to science, there are, according to the Vedic literature, higher order laws that govern the interactions of conscious entities. These laws are collectively known as *karma*. In the Vedic literature, *karma* is described in terms of actions and reactions. For example, if one causes unnecessary suffering to another living entity, one will undergo suffering in return. This suffering may come as environmental problems. One might counter that environmental problems can be explained in terms of observable human behavior. But why do people persist in such behavior, even when they know the results are undesirable? The action of *karma* on human consciousness may be an explanation.

One might ask if there is any scientific evidence for the law of *karma*. A likely place to look for such evidence would be in branches of science that deal with consciousness.

After studying the brain, Nobel laureate Roger Sperry suggested that the scientific principle of causation has to be broadened: "We have to recognize . . . different levels and types of causation, including higher kinds of causal control involving mental and vital forces that materialistic science has always rejected." He spoke of "a sequence of conscious or subconscious processes that have their own higher laws and dynamics."[2]

Sperry is not alone in his suggestion that we consider higher laws related to consciousness. Danish nuclear physicist Niels Bohr, also a Nobel laureate, stated, "All of us know that there is such a thing as consciousness, simply because we have it ourselves. Hence consciousness must be a part of nature, or, more generally, of reality, which means that quite apart from the laws of physics and chemistry, as laid down in quantum theory, we must consider laws of quite a different kind."[3]

Along the same lines, physicist David Bohm says, "The possibility is always open that there may exist an unlimited variety of additional properties, qualities, entities, systems, levels, etc., to which apply correspondingly new kinds of laws of nature."[4]

The law of *karma,* integral to India's Vedic philosophy, would be one example of such "new" laws. Although *karma* might not be exactly what Sperry, Bohr, or Bohm had in mind, it does not violate the general principles they outline in the above passages. Huston Smith, a former professor of philosophy at the Massachusetts Institute of Technology in the United States, said about *karma,* "Science has alerted the Western world to the importance of causal relationships in the physical world. Every physical event, we are inclined to believe, has its causes, and every cause will have its determinate effects. India extends this concept of universal causation to include man's moral and spiritual life as well."[5] *Karma* plays a leading role in the world's drift toward environmental catastrophe, and a large part of this *karma* is generated by unnecessary killing.

Meat and Karma

Each day millions of animals are routinely killed. People

fail to respect them as conscious entities with a right to live out their normal span of life.

Unfortunately, many scientists and philosophers have trouble recognizing consciousness even in human beings, what to speak of animals. Even people who admit that humans are conscious have trouble thinking of animals as anything other than robotlike biological machines.

But as Donald R. Griffin says in his book *Animal Thinking,* published by Harvard University Press: "It may be logically impossible to disprove the proposition that all other animals are thoughtless robots, but we can escape from this paralytic dilemma by relying on the same criteria of reasonable plausibility that lead us to accept the reality of consciousness in other people."[6]

As we have seen, scientific studies of near-death experiences indicate that consciousness in human beings can operate outside the physical mechanism of the body. This suggests the existence of a distinct unit of consciousness that is not simply a product of brain chemistry. In Sanskrit, this unit of consciousness is called the *ātmā,* or soul. If humans have souls, it is reasonable to suppose that animals also have them. Therefore, it is as wrong to kill an animal as it is to kill a human.

But when people needlessly kill millions of animals, there is something more than a sense of guilt to consider. There are karmic reactions, including degradation of the environment. *Ahimsā,* or nonviolence, as taught in many Eastern traditions, can therefore be beneficial for the environment.

Population and Karma

According to Malthus and his modern followers, population is almost always pushing the limit of available food. But according to India's Vedic teachings, the earth can always produce enough of life's necessities. According to this view, scarcity is not caused by overpopulation but by the negative *karma* generated by self-destructive actions of the planet's population.

People Working for Change

Lokanāth Swami

Lokanāth Swami is walking to bring about change. If he's not walking, he's probably driving a bullock cart. He began his *Padayātrā,* Sanskrit for "pilgrimage on foot," in India in 1984. Since then, *Padayātrā* walkers have crossed the length and breath of India three times, covering more than 30,000 kilometers (18,600 miles). Walkers range in number from twenty people (and five oxen) on remote roads to 100 in large cities and towns along the endless route. An elephant or two occasionally join the trekkers in India.

Born in Maharashtra, India, in 1949, Lokanāth is walking to prove that "a more natural way of life is both possible and easier." His method is to bring that way of life to where the people are.

After five years of walking in India, he decided to take *Padayātrā* abroad. He organized teams of walkers, usually with oxen (bullocks), and got them started, sometimes walking 500-mile routes. He became *Padayātrā's* principal organizer, worldwide spokesperson, and chief visionary, and he travels the world nonstop.

The walkers, or *padayātrīs,* teach that cows, bulls, and oxen are beautiful, useful, and friendly to human society. "If people insist on eating their flesh or using their skin for leather or other products, then why don't they at least wait

Śrīla Prabhupāda saw the world and its resources as God's energy, and these were not to be misused and wasted.

His Divine Grace
A. C. Bhaktivedanta Swami Prabhupāda
Founder-Ācārya of
The International Society for Krishna Consciousness

Mountains of rubbish have become symbolic of people who have more than they need. This is especially true in the industrialized nations, where the typical resident uses ten times more steel, twelve times more fuel, and fifteen times more paper than a typical resident of the developing nations.

Each person who becomes a vegetarian saves one acre of trees per year.

The meat industry is linked to deforestation, desertification, water pollution, water shortages, air pollution, and soil erosion.

Unrestricted hunting of animals for food, fur, or fun is threatening the existence of many species. About 1,000 are officially recognized as endangered. For example, during the 1980's, the number of African elephants shrank from 1.5 million to 600,000.

If people were to subsist on grains and other vegetarian foods alone, this would put far less strain on the earth's agricultural lands. About twenty vegetarians can be fed on the land that it takes to feed one meat eater.

This diet is not only healthier but also more satisfying to the mind and taste buds than meat-centered diets.

Most of our exposure to toxics comes from the air. While we drink two liters of water per day, we breathe 15–20 thousand liters of air. Motor vehicles are the world's biggest source of air pollution.

"We came to seek inspiration in Vṛndāvana's unique spiritual atmosphere and to experience firsthand a way of life that, despite the occasional loud tractor, still harmonizes with the natural rhythms and movements of mother nature."

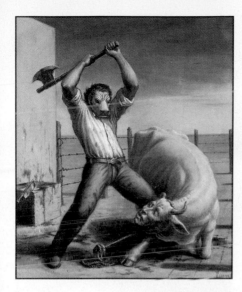

Karma plays a leading role in the world's drift toward environmental catastrophe and a large part of this karma is generated by unnecessary killing.

In countries such as Australia and the nations of Africa on the southern edge of the Sahara, cattle grazing and feed-crop production on marginal lands contribute substantially to desertification.

Central to ISKCON's self-sufficient farm communities is the use of draft animals, particularly oxen, or bullocks, as they are also called. This can ultimately free communities from dependence on machines and fossil fuels.

ISKCON's programs for protecting cows and harnessing ox power are intimately connected with its spiritual vegetarian diet.

The most toxic waste is nuclear waste, and its safe disposal is a problem that has yet to be solved. Nuclear plants in the United States are holding in temporary storage over 15,000 metric tons of high-level waste, which will remain harmful to human beings for about 250,000 years.

By 1994, the Mayapura project was producing most of its own grains, vegetables, fruits, and milk. Oxen are used for tilling the land and for transportation.

During a visit to India, Śrīla Prabhupāda urged his Indian-born disciple Lokanāth Swami to travel from village to village with ox carts instead of motor vehicles.

The temporary natural beauty of this world, in the form of flowing, pure rivers, forests full of trees bearing fruits and flowers, and mountains with cooling waterfalls, is, according to the Vedic literature, a reflection of the eternal divine nature.

till the animal dies?" asks Lokanāth. "Why kill them? Killing cows and bulls is brutal, and there's not a single good reason for it.

"I suppose I always knew this because my parents and family were religiously minded. But when I became a full-time Kṛṣṇa devotee, I made a commitment to deeply study Lord Kṛṣṇa and help educate people about the Kṛṣṇa culture."

Lokanāth's worldwide walkers convey more than cow culture. They also sing the names of Kṛṣṇa as they walk, distribute literature and spiritual food, and conduct evening programs in the cities, towns, and villages they visit.

By 1993 *Padayātrā* devotees were walking in over 30 countries, including Britain, India, the U.S.A., Mexico, Australia, the Philippines, Fiji, Spain, New Zealand, and Russia.

Lokanath stresses the simplicity of the original Kṛṣṇa culture. In 1993, the New Zealand *Padayātrā* promoted the environmental benefits of what Lokanāth calls "an agrarian civilization based on cow protection." "Walking for a Change" was the slogan for the 120-mile walk. That message has increasingly become a general theme for promoting *Padayātrā* worldwide, as representing "a more natural way of life" and "simple living and high thinking."

At evening programs in schools, community centers, churches, theaters, and town halls worldwide, *padayātris* present a complete picture of a God-centered society. Says Lokanāth, "We try to help people understand that we need a transcendental approach to solving the problems of the world. *Padayātrā* is a glimpse into the future life of this planet. Some of our most important values have been lost to the blind pursuit of material comforts. *Padayātrā* reminds us that real happiness can be found in simplicity, living close to nature and the animals, being easily satisfied with basic needs, and understanding that life should be God-centered. People of the world need to learn how to grow locally and eat locally."

The science of ecology has awakened us to a greater appreciation of how different organisms and natural resources are linked together in complex interdependency, and how easily this equilibrium can be upset—as in the case of acid rain. While doing research for NASA, America's space agency, scientist Jim Lovelock concluded that the "Earth's living matter, air, oceans, and land surface form a complex system which can be seen as a single organism and which has the capacity to keep our planet a fit place for life."[7] He calls his hypothesis the Gaia principle, after the Greek goddess of the earth.

Lovelock says, "The concept of Mother Earth, or, as the Greeks called her long ago, Gaia, has been widely held throughout history and has been the basis of a belief which still coexists with the great religions."[8] India's books of Vedic knowledge state that the earth is the visible form of the goddess Bhūmi, who restricts or increases her productive capacity according to the population's level of spiritual consciousness.

"Therefore," states Śrīla Prabhupāda, "although there may be a great increase in population on the surface of the earth, if the people are exactly in line with God consciousness . . . such a burden on the earth is a source of pleasure for her."[9] If people are God conscious, then there is no artificial limit to the population the earth can comfortably support.

Margaret Sanger (1879–1966), a principal organizer of the modern birth control movement, believed that "women should free themselves from biological slavery, which could best be accomplished through birth control."[10] The *Vedas,* however, inform us about the cycle of birth and death, in which everyone, man or woman, is caught up. That is also a form of "biological slavery."

By nature, we are eternal (birthless and deathless) spirit souls. But now we are encaged in material bodies subject to various miseries and the destructive influence of time. In other words, we are involved in reincarnation, transmigration of the soul from one material body into another, lifetime after lifetime. Real birth control means stopping perpetual rebirth.

But the laws of *karma* state that if people engage in birth control methods such as abortion, then they are insuring their future bondage. Śrīla Prabhupāda warns, "In the next life they also enter the womb of a mother and are killed in the same way."[11] And as for the soul denied birth by abortion or contraception, it must also enter another womb. Birth control thus fails, because ultimately it prevents not one birth. So to prevent the pain of repeated birth for both parent and child, something other than material birth control is required—the development of spiritual consciousness, which includes spiritual birth control.

Such birth control can be accomplished in two ways — by practicing celibacy or spiritually-motivated sex to produce a child that is wanted. For most people, lifetime celibacy is not a viable option. A more realistic option is a marriage in which the partners practice voluntary restraint until they desire to have children.

This system of birth control does not mean no sex and fewer people but proper sex and better people, be they few or many. In this regard, Malthus made a point worth noting: "I have never considered any possible increase of population as an evil, except as far as it might increase the proportion of vice and misery."[12]

If the population is good, then no matter how numerous they will be able to cooperate with each other peacefully and with the blessings of God receive ample resources from Mother Earth. A population of good character will not generate as much "vice and misery," and this is desirable for the health of the environment. Most environmental problems can be traced to human vices, especially greed.

Further, the law of *karma* holds that the natural order is disturbed when the biological development of any living being, in or out of the womb, is terminated. Such termination of the natural development of a living being reflects selfishness and lack of compassion, which can be seen as a kind of pollution of human consciousness. The link between pollution of consciousness and pollution of the environment is something that bears careful consideration.

Freedom from Karma by Mantra Meditation

The force of *karma* keeps people trapped in the destructive patterns of consciousness responsible for our planetary crisis. Under the control of *karma,* people instinctively pursue material gratifications and possessions, thus fueling the overconsuming economy that overwhelms the environment with pollution of all kinds.

The subtle, destructive energies of *karma* can, however, be overcome. The law of *karma* acts most powerfully on those who identify the self totally as the material body and mind instead of the soul. By becoming free from such identification, people can become free from the control of *karma.*

This requires a change of behavior. Originally, the conscious self has its origin in the supreme conscious self. Great spiritual teachers in the Vedic tradition therefore advise that we reconnect ourselves with that supreme person to be completely free from *karma.* This can be done through devotional spiritual practices.

The *Vedas* explain that powerful spiritual energies can be generated by *yoga,* meditation, and chanting of *mantras.* In the present age, the chanting of *mantras* is particularly effective. When properly chanted, the combinations of sounds in *mantras* release their energies. The most powerful *mantras,* according to the *Vedas,* are those composed of names of God, such as the Hare Kṛṣṇa *mantra:* Hare Kṛṣṇa, Hare Kṛṣṇa, Kṛṣṇa Kṛṣṇa, Hare Hare/ Hare Rāma, Hare Rāma, Rāma Rāma, Hare Hare. The *Vedas* teach that God's name, being nondifferent from God Himself, is supremely potent. Therefore, by properly chanting the Hare Kṛṣṇa *mantra,* one can be freed from karmic reactions. The chanting of the Hare Kṛṣṇa *mantra* is especially effective when people chant it aloud together. This form of meditation reduces *karma*, which is one of the root causes of our environmental crisis.

7
Rural Communities of ISKCON

"Our farm projects are an extremely important part of our movement. We must become self-sufficient by growing our own grains and producing our own milk. There will be no question of poverty. They should be developed as an ideal society dependent on natural products, not industry."

Śrīla Prabhupāda
Letter, December 18, 1974

Human priorities are out of balance. The scientific and technological revolutions of the past few centuries have given us a way of life that is destructive of both human values and the environment.

But what new direction shall humanity take, as it moves toward what some call the postindustrial era? Economist Robert Heilbroner says, "I believe the long-term solution requires nothing less than the gradual abandonment of the lethal techniques, the uncongenial lifeways, and the dangerous mentality of industrial civilization itself."[1] This would imply "the end of the giant factory, the huge office, perhaps of the urban complex."[2]

Such a postindustrial civilization would be primarily agrarian, emphasizing local production and self-sufficiency. At present not many people may be attracted to this way of life. "The best that can be hoped for," observes Alan Durning of the World Watch Institute, "is a gradual widening of the circle of those practicing voluntary simplicity."[3]

The International Society for Krishna Consciousness (ISKCON) is one organization that is trying to gradually widen that circle of voluntary simplicity. Over the past twenty-five years, the Society has established more than forty rural communities worldwide. Individual members of ISKCON, using their own resources, have established additional smaller communities. These agrarian communities are not merely places for growing crops and herding animals. They are communities in the full sense, with many supporting arts, crafts, and appropriate technologies. They are also centers of spiritual culture, providing the nonmaterial satisfaction that is essential for solving the environmental crisis. Now under construction in Māyāpur, West Bengal, is a model international township for 25,000 people. None of these communities has yet reached the goal of sustainable self-sufficiency, but they are moving in that direction, some more rapidly than others. Progress is often slow, and there are many obstacles, but at least an effort is being made.

Ox Power

Central to ISKCON's self-sufficient farm communities is the use of draft animals, particularly oxen, or bullocks, as they are also called. This can ultimately free communities from dependence on machines and fossil fuels.

Two members of the Kṛṣṇa consciousness movement working in the area of ox power are the husband-wife team of Balabhadra Dāsa and Chāyā Dāsī (Bill and Irene Dove), founders of the International Society for Cow Protection (ISCOWP), based in the U.S.A. ("People Working for Change," p. 76).

"ISCOWP is primarily concerned with presenting alternatives to present agricultural practices that support and depend upon the meat industry," says Balabhadra. "A lacto-vegetarian diet, cruelty-free lifetime protection of the cow, ox training, alternative energies offered by the cow and ox, and a sound ecological, agrarian life-style are the practices that ISCOWP would like to make available to everyone." ISCOWP supports organic gardening of vegetables, spices, grains, and fruits, making use of local seed banks and natural methods of pest control, and encourages crafts such as blacksmithing, weaving, spinning, and broom making. In pursuance of these goals they are networking with several organizations, including Beyond Beef of Washington, D.C., the Bharatiya Cattle Resource Development Foundation (New Delhi, India), Tillers International, and the American Vedic Association.

Balabhadra and Chāyā urge potential farmers to start small, family farms powered by oxen. In 1991, the couple established a 3.5 acre demonstration farm near Efland, North Carolina, which will serve, Balabhadra says, as "a living classroom setting for educational seminars emphasizing ox training and ox-powered field work." Balabhadra and Chāyā also travel across the U. S. with a team of trained oxen, showing them at fairs, festivals, and other events.

On May 24, 1974, Śrīla Prabhupāda spoke about the advantages of ox-powered transportation with some of his students in Rome, Italy. After hearing the effects of the oil crisis following the 1973 Mideast war, he said, "Petrol is required for transport, but if you are localized, there is no question of transport. You don't require petrol. . . . The oxen will solve the problem of transport."

Later, during a visit to India, Śrīla Prabhupāda urged his Indian-born disciple Lokanāth Swami to travel from village to village with oxcarts instead of motor vehicles (see People Working for Change, p.58).

Lokanāth Swami then organized a *Padayātrā* ("pilgrimage on foot") that continues to travel the length and breadth of India several times, going from village to village and town to town with oxcarts and exhibits. In each village and town, the members of the party are well received, attracting considerable attention to their message of living a simple, God-conscious life in harmony with nature's laws. Lokanāth Swami has since begun *Padayātrās* in dozens of other countries.

People Working for Change

Priyavrata Dāsa Brahmacārī

The ecological crisis is a crisis of values, according to Priyavrata Dāsa Brahmachari (Paul Turner), global coordinator of the Hare Kṛṣṇa Food for Life (FFL) program. In 1978, Australian devotees began a mobile FFL service in Sydney's Hyde Park, which grew to feed 1,900 *karma*-free spiritual vegetarian meals a week to hungry and homeless people in seven cities throughout the country.

"The uneven distribution of food in Australia, and the whole world for that matter," says Priyavrata, "is due not to food shortages but to greed. Much too much land is being exploited for cash crops—junk foods, exports, tobacco, and alcohol. Agribusiness is destroying small farms, food prices are soaring, and soil and forests are disappearing fast. Food has to be returned to the hands of the people. We want to set an example for environmentalists."

A sprawling farm in Millfield, New South Wales, was an appropriate setting for his original headquarters. From this 500-acre spread, dedicated to Kṛṣṇa consciousness and sustainable organic agriculture, Priyavrata produced a quarterly newsletter on a Macintosh computer.

Now he travels throughout the world, visiting Hare Kṛṣṇa Food for Life distribution centers such as those in London, Moscow, Sydney, Los Angeles, and Belgrade. Using a laptop computer, he continues to produce his newsletter, sending it out worldwide every two months.

Priyavrata's vegetarian food relief campaign in Australia, a nation that produces large quantities of beef, could have proven controversial. But government authorities there see the food as nutritious. Bob Brown, member of the Australian parliament and Federal Minister for Land Transport, described it as "a healthy diet"; state parliament member Bob Carr of New South Wales said Hare Kṛṣṇa Food for Life is more than just a free food program: "It is a commitment to improve the quality of life." In 1991, Reverend Ted Noffs, Sydney's renowned antidrug campaigner, cited Hare Kṛṣṇa Food for Life as "the real spiritual work of this city and the real welfare work, because it's not just a hand-out." John C. Price, another New South Wales parliament member, said that the aims of the program were "certainly reconcilable with basic Christian and humanitarian practice."

Priyavrata says that Hare Kṛṣṇa Food for Life volunteers throughout the world care deeply because they see the bigger picture. "The environment is a mess because we're conditioned to see the earth and its creatures as things to be exploited unlimitedly for personal gratification."

A goal of the Kṛṣṇa consciousness movement, stated in its original and still current charter, is to "check the imbalance of values in life and achieve real unity and peace in the world." Written in 1965 by the founder of the Kṛṣṇa society, A.C. Bhaktivedanta Swami Prabhupāda, these words are still the guiding principle of Hare Kṛṣṇa Food for Life.

Says Priyavrata: "Our goal is to help correct this imbalance of values and ensure that no one in the world goes hungry. There's an almost unconscious drive to have and enjoy more than we really need. This compulsion generates a callousness and negligence that's spread so widely now that much of the world goes to bed hungry at night. The same syndrome also lies at the root of the environmental crisis. It's not so easy for most people to identify this ultimate cause, because it happens to be spiritual in nature."

A Meatless, Karma-Free Diet

ISKCON's programs of cow protection and ox power are intimately connected with its spiritual vegetarian diet. The beef industry is one of the major causes of environmental destruction worldwide. Saving cows and bulls from the slaughterhouse is, therefore, one of the main things we can do to improve the environment. Here are some of the ways the International Society for Krishna Consciousness is helping spread meatless, *karma*-free eating.

First of all, the Kṛṣṇa consciousness movement has more than 50 restaurants in 20 countries. These restaurants serve only *prasādam,* vegetarian food that has been prepared with love and devotion for the pleasure of the Supreme Lord, Kṛṣṇa. In the *Bhagavad-gītā,* the Lord says that one should eat only food that has first been offered to Him. He further states that He will accept only vegetarian foods. If one offers the Lord such vegetarian foods, one becomes free from any *karma* involved in taking the lives of plants. And according to Vedic teachings, one also obtains a positive spiritual benefit from eating *prasādam.*

Karma-free vegetarian meals are also served at all of the more than 300 Kṛṣṇa consciousness centers around the world, as well as at hundreds of major public festivals each year. We estimate that the Kṛṣṇa consciousness movement has served over 900 million *prasādam* meals since 1966. Furthermore, hundreds of thousands of Kṛṣṇa worshipers prepare *prasādam* meals in their homes.

Former Beatle George Harrison, a long-time friend of the Kṛṣṇa consciousness movement, once said, "It's a pity you don't have restaurants or temples on all the main streets of every little town and village like those hamburger and fried chicken places. You should put them out of business."

Over the years, ISKCON has worked with many organizations, including the Farm Animal Reform Movement, to promote *karma*-free vegetarianism at events such as the Great

American Meat-Out, Earth Day, and World Vegetarian Day.

Members of the Kṛṣṇa consciousness movement have also authored a number of influential vegetarian cookbooks. *The Higher Taste,* which the authors of *Divine Nature* helped write, is a small paperback that combines a selection of recipes with a philosophical introduction to the Kṛṣṇa consciousness movement's *karma*-free spiritual vegetarian diet. It was especially designed to reach a wide audience, and to date over 10 million copies have been sold in several languages.

In 1988, Yamunā Devī Dāsī authored a compendium of Indian vegetarian cooking titled *Lord Kṛṣṇa's Cuisine* (see "People Working for Change," p. 16). It was the first vegetarian cookbook ever to win the prestigious Best Cookbook of the Year award from the International Association of Cooking Professionals. The *Chicago Tribune* newspaper called it "the Taj Mahal of cookbooks." In 1992, Yamunā came out with another prize-winning cookbook, *Yamuna's Table,* and she has also become a regular contributor to the cooking pages of the *Washington Post,* one of the most widely read newspapers in the U.S.

In 1990, Kurma Dāsa, an accomplished cook who operates Hare Kṛṣṇa restaurants in Melbourne, Australia, came out with a cookbook titled *Great Vegetarian Dishes.* He also appears in a 13-part television series called *Cooking with Kurma,* which has reached millions of viewers throughout the world.

Other members of ISKCON have also published cookbooks. And ISKCON Television (ITV) has produced videos on cow protection and the Hare Kṛṣṇa movement's spiritual vegetarian diet.

ISKCON members regularly lecture on the environmental advantages of a spiritual vegetarian diet in their cooking classes. These classes are held in private homes, colleges and universities, and in ISKCON's temples, restaurants, and rural communities throughout the world.

In addition to cookbooks, the message of avoiding meat is found in all of the books of Vedic philosophy published by the Bhaktivedanta Book Trust. These publications, with over 400 million copies sold, reinforce basic spiritual messages that can help reverse the rush toward environmental disaster.

The Food for Life program distributes nourishing *prasādam* meals to the homeless, hungry, and disadvantaged throughout the world, in cities such as Calcutta, Bombay, Nairobi, Durban, São Paulo, Lima, New York, Philadelphia, Belgrade, Berlin, London, Zurich, Moscow, Riga, Kiev, Warsaw, and Budapest. In addition to distributing *karma*-free vegetarian meals through its regular outlets, Hare Kṛṣṇa Food for Life also participates in disaster relief, as in the massive floods that hit Bengal in 1977 and the earthquakes that struck Armenia in 1989 and India in 1993.

Hare Kṛṣṇa Food for Life cooperates with government and private relief agencies worldwide, including the Red Cross, UNICEF, United Way, Adventists Services (Sarajevo, Bosnia-Herzegovina), the British Ministry of Agriculture's Intervention Board, Taskforce for Social Services (Belgrade), Caritas, and the Federal Emergency Management Administration and Department of Agriculture of the United States Government.

Hare Kṛṣṇa Food for Life volunteers emphasize the environmental benefits of the spiritual vegetarian food they distribute. As a long-term solution to world hunger, Hare Kṛṣṇa Food for Life advocates the following: a return to self-sufficient rural communities based on cow protection, the ending of the wasteful and environmentally destructive meat industry, a return to God-conscious spiritual values, and the adoption of a diet of *prasādam*.

Village Life

In a postindustrial world, the self-sufficient agricultural village, rather than the urban factory or rural factory farm, will be the primary economic unit.

"Our farm projects are an extremely important part of our movement," said Śrīla Prabhupāda in a letter dated December 18, 1974. "We must become self-sufficient by growing our own grains and producing our own milk. There will be no question of poverty. They should be developed as an ideal society dependent on natural products, not industry. . . . Let everyone chant Hare Kṛṣṇa, eat nicely, and keep the body fit and healthy. This is ideal life-style."

Near Carriere, Mississippi, in the United States, about 20 families reside at the Kṛṣṇa consciousness movement's New Tālavana community. Members use 1,300 acres for timber, pasture, and crops.

In 1975, Śrīla Prabhupāda advised the community to strive for self-sufficiency. The members of New Talavana should grow their own grain, fruit, and vegetables, said Śrīla Prabhupāda. They should keep a few cows for milk, which they could then turn into yogurt, butter, and fresh natural cheese. They should use oxen to plow the fields and for local transport. They should grow sugarcane for sweetener. They should grow castor beans and use the oil to burn in lamps. They should grow cotton, spin it into thread, and weave their own cloth on handlooms. For building materials, they should use logs and bricks. Finally, Śrīla Prabhupāda encouraged the residents of New Tālavana to build a magnificent temple at the center of the community.

Later that year, Śrīla Prabhupāda visited New Tālavana and gave additional advice about how to organize the community. "Avoid machines. Keep everyone employed as a *brāhmaṇa* [teacher], *kṣatriya* [administrator], *vaiśya* [farm owner or merchant], or *śūdra* [laborer]. Nobody should sit idle." He was explaining the Vedic social system, with its natural divisions or classes that allow people to make the most of their special aptitudes and inclinations.

"The *brāhmaṇas*," said Śrīla Prabhupāda, "study transcendental literature such as *Bhagavad-gītā* and the *Upaniṣads*. And they lecture and instruct, as well as worship the Deity in the temple. They should have ideal character," he said, "and the other classes provide food and shelter out of appreciation for their guidance." The *kṣatriyas,* taking advice from the *brāhmaṇas,* manage and govern the village; also, they apportion land to the *vaiśyas.* The *vaiśyas* use the land to produce grains, fruits, and vegetables, and to raise cows for milk. They give 25% of their produce or earnings to the *kṣatriyas,* who utilize it for village projects. The *śūdras,* the artisans and craftspeople, assist the other three classes.

The current residents of New Tālavana have not achieved self-sufficiency and have only partially introduced the Vedic social system. But they are working in that direction.

In August 1976, Śrīla Prabhupāda visited New Māyāpur, ISKCON's farm community near Luçay-le-Mâle in central France. As elsewhere, Prabhupāda stressed self-sufficiency, advising members to build cottages with wood from the forests on their land, keep cows, and grow vegetables, grains, fruits, and flowers. "Try to concentrate on this village organization," he said.

As of 1991, the ISKCON farm at Almviks Gärd, thirty-six kilometers from Stockholm, Sweden, was home to 13 families, a total of 41 adults and 8 children. There were also 5 milking cows, 6 oxen, and 19 young or unproductive cows. About 55 of the 165 acres are under cultivation. Crops include hay, wheat, oats, rye, potatoes, carrots, beet roots, cabbage, fruit trees (apple, pear, plum, cherry), and flowers. The community also has bee hives. Devotees carefully harvest wood from about 110 acres of forest and use it for construction. In addition, the community has its own school, bakery, and handlooms. Residents grow crops from local seeds and train oxen for plowing and hauling. They say, "Our aim is to give an example of Kṛṣṇa conscious life and economic self-sufficiency." There is a guest room for visitors.

In Poland, there is an ISKCON farm community near the

town of Czarnow (See "People Working for Change," p. 24). Called New Śāntipur, it occupies 100 acres. Members also rent another 150 acres from the government. New Śāntipur is home to about 60 people. They use oxen for much of the farm work.

As of 1991, 7 families were living at the 1,700-acre Śaraṇāgati Dhāma farm, twenty miles from the small town of Ashcroft in the mountains of British Columbia, Canada. The community offers 5-acre lifetime leases to members, transferable to their children. Currently, there are 5 acres of hay, 200 acres of pasture, and 2 acres of organic vegetables. Two cows and 4 oxen make up the community's small herd. Lumber from trees on the farm is used for construction. Some residents aim to farm without machines. Others use machinery, but on a small scale.

The ISKCON farm at Gītā-Nāgarī (named after a model community envisioned by Śrīla Prabhupāda in 1948) is located near Port Royal, Pennsylvania, U.S.A. Of 325 acres, 150 are under cultivation for animal feed, and a 5-acre organic garden supplies the community with a variety of vegetables. A few cows are milked and a few oxen are trained, and the farm is also home to about a hundred nonmilking cows and nonworking oxen. Originally, the community operated as a commercial dairy but is now making a difficult transition to local self-sufficiency.

In December of 1976, Śrīla Prabhupāda visited ISKCON's 600-acre farming community near Hyderabad, in south central India. By means of this community, Śrīla Prabhupāda hoped to revive spiritually centered village life, which has been on the decline in India. Giving up their traditional culture and values, many village dwellers have gone to the cities to work in factories.

"Let them come here, live peacefully, eat sumptuously, get all the other necessities of life, and become Kṛṣṇa conscious," said Śrīla Prabhupāda during his December 1976 visit.

One hundred and forty men, women, and children live at the Kṛṣṇa consciousness movement's Nova Gokula farm near Pindamonhangaba, in the Mantiquiera Mountains 114 miles northeast of São Paulo, Brazil. Residents of Nova Gokula have planted 500 orange trees, 50 mango trees, 500 papaya trees, 5,000 banana trees, and many grape vines. Cultivated land includes 20 acres of corn, 10 acres of barley, 5 acres of green vegetables, 2 acres of dhal (lentils), 10 acres of cow fodder, and 10 acres of rice. There are also 185 acres of pasture for Nova Gokula's 56 cows, bulls, and calves.

Members also grow flowers. Guru Dāsa, the development director of Nova Gokula (see "People Working for Change," p. 4), says, "Several species of orchids that grow here are considered endangered species, so we are cultivating them to save them."

Nova Gokula is located in an important watershed region for the Paraiba River. "Our efforts to improve the watershed are good for the whole region," says Guru Dāsa. "Two years ago, we wrote up our plan to preserve the area and the water. We presented it to the city of Pindamonhangaba, and they were very enthusiastic about it."

About half the land at Nova Gokula is set aside for a "Vedic Village" centered on cow protection and complete self-sufficiency, with family farms as the basic economic units. On the other half, there is a community that still relies on machine technology and has contact with the outside economy.

ISKCON's New Nandagram farm community occupies 265 acres of forest and grassy range near Melbourne, Australia. Established in 1987, the community has grown to 23 members, with another 20 living nearby. (see "People Working for Change," p. 50)

For planning the future development of New Nandagram, members sought the help of David Holmgren, a founder of the "permaculture" concept of sustainable agriculture. Holmgren worked with farm manager Gokula Dāsa to produce a 50-page study that shows how New Nandagram can become a self-sufficient community based on cow protection.

An important part of the plan was determining how many animals the acreage could sustain. His findings showed that New Nandagram can support 1 cow for every 2 acres. With somewhat less than 200 acres available for agricultural use, New Nandagram could support about 90 bovines, based on a 15-year life span for each animal. He calculated that a maximum of 6 cows a year could be milked. But this number can supply milk for the entire community.

"Making use of the bullocks as work animals should be a key element in making the farm efficient and sustainable within the religious constraints," adds Holmgren.

Because the farm's spring water has an unpleasant taste, Holmgrem recommended rainwater collection for human drinking. The community therefore built rooftop systems to capture rainwater.

The development plan calls for the planting of over 50,000 trees, specially selected to provide fodder for cows and attract insect-eating birds to garden areas. Forest will cover 40% of the farm's acreage.

Holmgren proposed using oxen to haul cut logs to a portable sawmill. "Working bullocks harvesting timber could become a major environmental education attraction demonstrating sustainable farm forestry techniques while reinforcing the traditional Hare Kṛṣṇa relationship to cows," said Holmgren.

New Nandagram is one of the few ISKCON rural communities with this complete a plan for self-sufficiency. Although attainment of self-sufficiency may be many years, or even decades, away, the plan is based on sound principles and is being executed step by step.

Australian ISKCON members also intend to introduce permaculture concepts at their 600-acre farm (New Gokula) near Sydney and their 1,000-acre farm (New Govardhana) near Brisbane.

People Working for Change

Irene Dove (Chāyā Dāsī)

"You and I know the bull is a person with feelings just like us," says Irene Dove, codirector of ISCOWP. The acronym stands for the International Society for Cow Protection.

Irene, her husband William Dove (Balabhadra Dāsa), and two oxen travel coast-to-coast across the U.S.A., teaching the public about the gentleness of cows and oxen and the environmental, physical, and economic benefits of cow protection.

Oxen, Irene says, can still be the most effective and economical way for small family farmers to plow crops and haul goods. She explains that gas derived from bovine manure can be used to power electrical generators for "appropriate" or "intermediate" technology, and that oxen yoked to a large axle can drive purpose-built irrigation systems.

Born in Long Island, New York, in 1946, Irene joined the Hare Kṛṣṇa religion full-time in 1969. In 1980 she moved to the 325-acre Kṛṣṇa community of Gītā-Nāgarī, near Harrisburg, Pennsylvania, where she spent 11 years teaching in the community's school system. When she moved onto the farm, it was launching what was probably the world's first "Adopt-a-Cow" program. Members paid a fee to adopt a calf, and the program administrators agreed to protect the animal from the slaughterhouse throughout its entire lifetime.

While living at Gītā-Nāgarī, Irene's interest in schooling children gradually transformed into educating adults about cow protection. She got involved in Adopt-a-Cow and began displaying live cows and bullocks at dozens of farm exhibitions and other public events. When she saw "thousands of people undergo a dramatic change of heart" toward protecting cows, her enthusiasm became a life commitment. Irene and Bill started thinking about how to protect cows throughout the world and decided to organize a worldwide network of small farms pledged to such a program.

In 1991, they moved to a 3.5-acre farm in Efland, North Carolina, where they officially launched ISCOWP. Irene and Bill are developing this farm as a prototype and educational resource center for cow protection and ox-power. They teach people how to build wooden yokes for plowing and hauling, and how to make wooden gears which can be used to produce a variety of simple machines.

"Numbers can prove that for small American farms bovine power systems are more cost efficient than tractors," says Irene. She adds wittily, "Anyone who properly uses alternative ox-based energy will discover that bull calves become the backbone, not the soup bone, of the American farm."

Irene and Bill have started an international organization to develop the concept of small farms based on cow protection. Their "International Farm Network" project began in 1992. Several small farmers have joined the program, adding cow protection to an existing farm or starting one based on ISCOWP principles.

ISCOWP's outreach program includes schoolchildren. For $10, a "junior member" can join and become entitled to a quarterly junior newsletter containing coloring and writing contests.

"People are always amazed that my 15-year-old daughter Lakshmī, who weighs in at about 110 pounds, has such an affectionate relationship with our ox, Gītā. She totally controls this 800-pound animal with voice commands."

In 1993, residents of the Śaraṇāgati community in Canada hosted a two-week-long permaculture conference. One of the major workshops was an exercise to design a permaculture plan for the settlement. The event was considered a milestone for ISKCON community development.

Sustainable Small Towns

In a postindustrial world, there would still be towns, although they would be smaller than those of today. They might resemble the cities of Renaissance Europe. Florence, for example, at the height of its cultural ascendancy, had only 35,000 to 45,000 inhabitants.

As early as 1948, in an essay titled *Interpretations of Bhagavad-gītā*, Śrīla Prabhupāda outlined his vision for a town-sized, self-sufficient community based on the spiritual teachings of the *Bhagavad-gītā*. He called the planned community Gītā-Nāgarī, the city of the *Bhavagad-gītā*. "The Gītā-Nāgarī shall set the example that neither God nor the living being nor nature is in any way antagonistic toward one another, but that all of them exist in harmony as a complete whole unit," said Śrīla Prabhupāda.

The spiritual center of the community would be a temple dedicated to Lord Kṛṣṇa, who spoke the timeless teachings of the *Bhagavad-gītā* to His friend and devotee Arjuna. The community would also include an educational institution called the Gītā School. "The children of the inhabitants of Gītā-Nāgarī shall get free education with the facility of free boarding and free lodging in this institution," said Śrīla Prabhupāda.

Students and retired persons would carry out the duties of worship, teaching, writing, and publishing. Other members, principally the married adults, would see to economic development (especially cow protection and agriculture) and government.

In 1970, Śrīla Prabhupāda initiated construction of a spiritual township modeled on the Gītā Nāgarī principle. He chose as the location Māyāpur, in West Bengal.

Māyāpur has a special spiritual significance for the members of the Kṛṣṇa consciousness movement. It was here that Śrī Caitanya Mahāprabhu, renowned as an incarnation of God, appeared in 1486. Śrī Caitanya spread the chanting of the Hare Kṛṣṇa *mantra* all over India and requested His followers to spread it to every town and village in the world.

Today, the central features of Māyāpur city, now home to several hundred full-time residents, are a Kṛṣṇa temple and a domed memorial to Śrīla Prabhupāda. There are also three major guesthouses, capable of accommodating 1,200 visitors. These are surrounded by lush, well-tended parks and gardens. Between 1982 and 1992, 12 million people visited this spiritual center.

By 1994, the Māyāpur project was producing most of its own grains, vegetables, fruits, and milk. Oxen are used for some tilling of the land and for some transportation.

To provide cotton cloth for residents and others, the Māyāpur project has 45 handlooms. Residents also grow flowers for temple worship and have started a number of cottage industries in addition to weaving. They publish books and magazines, using a printing press located on the property.

Eventually, the Māyāpur town is expected to house 25,000 residents. It will be organized according to the Vedic social system called *varṇāśrama,* with its divisions of teachers, administrators, businessmen and farmers, and laborers. Most people rightly deplore India's present caste system, which is based on birth. But the original *varṇāśrama* system, as described in the *Bhagavad-gītā* and other works of Vedic literature, is based not on birth but on qualification.

Like the Gītā-Nāgarī township envisioned by Śrīla Prabhupāda in 1948, the Māyāpur town will have a grand temple, including a planetarium exhibiting the cosmology that underlies Vedic civilization and culture. This temple will be completed early in the twenty-first century. It will be large enough to hold 10,000 people at a time.

The entire city will be arranged around the temple, in the manner suggested by urban planning directions found in the *Vedas*. Vedic city planners knew how to locate temples, residences, parks, agricultural fields, and markets in a way that fosters social and spiritual harmony. Close to the central temple complex will be places of culture and education. Next will come places for living and working. Finally, there will be an outer circle of farms, which will provide enough food for all the residents.

Opportunities for Involvement

As can be seen, not all of the programs of the Kṛṣṇa consciousness movement are unique. What is unique is the combination of all these programs—self-sufficient sustainable rural communities and small towns, an emphasis on spiritual values and cultivation of nonmaterial sources of happiness, a God-centered cosmology, cow protection and ox power, and a spiritually oriented vegetarian diet—in one voluntary, administratively decentralized international association. There are many opportunities for involvement and exchange of views, and these are listed in the directory at the end of this book.

8

The Environment of the Soul

"So, everthing in the spiritual world is substantial and original. This material world is only an imitation. Whatever we see in the material world is all imitation, shadow. . . . Whatever beautiful thing we see in this material world is simply an imitation of the real beauty of the spiritual world."[1]

Śrīla Prabhupāda
The Journey of Self-Discovery

Seeing that the world is heading toward environmental catastrophe, most people are trying to deal with the problem—on a material level. But these efforts are only part of the solution. They fail to address the underlying cause of the environmental crisis.

The world can never be perfect, but to restore it to a healthier condition, four elements are necessary:

(1) A new diet. The meat industry is one of the biggest causes of such environmental problems as deforestation, desertification, and air and water pollution. The grain-fed beef industry also diverts grain from human consumption, thus contributing substantially to world hunger. A vegetarian diet would therefore be a major step forward. Members of the Kṛṣṇa consciousness movement follow and teach a spiritual vegetarian diet (*prasādam*). Through 300 temples, 50 vegetarian restaurants, and other food programs such as Hare Kṛṣṇa Food for Life, they have distributed 900 million plates of *prasādam* since 1966. The Kṛṣṇa consciousness movement also promotes a vegetarian diet through books (including cookbooks), videos, and cooking classes.

(2) A spiritually based, God-conscious cosmology. The

People Working for Change

Ranchor Prime

In 1989, London resident Ranchor Prime became aware of impending ecological disaster in Vṛndāvana, one of India's important pilgrimage sites. As a devotee of Lord Kṛṣṇa, he decided to do something about it.

The town of Vṛndāvana, population 50,000, is the sacred place where Lord Kṛṣṇa displayed His divine pastimes fifty centuries ago. Vṛndāvana's temples, riverbanks, groves, and forests are visited by three million pilgrims annually.

As a regular visitor, Ranchor discovered Vṛndāvana's famous forests and groves were fast disappearing, its soil was eroding, and its sacred river Yamunā was becoming dangerously polluted. Environmental values embedded in Hindu scriptures seemed neglected, or sacrificed to creeping materialism.

In 1991, Ranchor convinced the World Wide Fund for Nature (WWF), based in Geneva, to provide funding for a three-year program to begin restoring the ecology of a region that hundreds of millions of people see as the most sacred spot on earth. On frequent trips to India, Ranchor has since helped to develop the "WWF Vrindavan Forest Revival Project," working hand in hand with WWF India and local residents.

The restoration effort centers on the Parikrama Path, the seven-mile route that encircles the town. It was once a shady forest path. But today few trees remain, and the sand on which pilgrims walk barefoot is often burning hot. Raw sewage and rubbish along the sacred walkway are commonplace. Ranchor regrets that developers have paved over much of the sandy path, leaving it covered with sharp stones and gravel, which often cut pilgrims' feet. Passing motor vehicles routinely force walkers off the road.

Ranchor convinced the International Society for Krishna Consciousness (ISKCON) to provide land along the Parikrama Path for the project's first phase: a nursery for trees and bushes of local origin. The WWF provided a well on this land, installed a water pump and irrigation system, and erected security fencing. Trained by project personnel, Vṛndāvana residents formed a plantation team. Two more nurseries have since been established on ground lent by other local institutions. Since 1992, trees and bushes have been planted along the walkway, forming a focus for widespread community action and education in the town. The plan is to renovate the entire path, dealing with Vṛndāvana's serious environmental problems in the process.

The long-term aim of the project is to focus public attention on Hinduism's traditional environmental values and on the importance of preserving them. WWF India workers see the project as one of their most significant and have committed themselves to supporting it for as long as it takes to create lasting changes.

Ranchor has now joined with other devotees of Kṛṣṇa to form Friends of Vrindavan, an international charity whose purpose is to protect and restore the numerous sacred groves spread throughout the Vṛndāvana region.

"The key to India's environmental problems is to be found in her own spiritual traditions," he says. "We want to help awaken Hindus to this important fact and at the same time save Vṛndāvana from disaster."

[For more information about Friends of Vrindavan, contact Ranchor Prime at 10 Grafton Mews, London W19 5LF, UK] godless world view of modern science portrays humans as soul-less biological machines. This encourages the domination and exploitation of the world's resources as the primary goal of life, which leads to the environmental degradation we see around us. But the cosmology drawn from India's Vedic literature shows that a mechanistic world view is mistaken in its denial of the soul and God. Vedic cosmology emphasizes self-realization as the primary goal of human life and thus encourages an environmentally sound life of natural simplicity. Through the Bhaktivedanta Institute, the Kṛṣṇa consciousness movement educates scholars and the general public about Vedic cosmology and its accompanying way of life.

(3) Sources of nonmaterial satisfaction. Many commentators have noted that the world's environmental problems will not be solved until people reduce their desires for material consumption. This is possible only if people gain tangible experience of superior forms of happiness and satisfaction. The Kṛṣṇa consciousness movement offers this through the practice of *bhakti-yoga,* and especially through Hare Kṛṣṇa *mantra* meditation.

(4) A new form of community. Urban-industrial lifeways are largely responsible for the environmental crisis. Many scholars and environmentalists therefore recommend a return to village life. In pursuit of this concept, the Kṛṣṇa consciousness movement has established more than 40 rural communities on 5 continents, all working towards local self-sufficiency. Well under way is a model town for 25,000 at Māyāpur, West Bengal. Cow protection and the use of oxen for agriculture and transport will largely free the Kṛṣṇa consciousness movement's rural communities from dependence on oil and machines produced in factories.

But even if we are somehow able to transform this planet into an environmental paradise, insurmountable problems will still exist. According to Vedic cosmology, the true environment of the soul is the spiritual dimension of reality. Souls that depart from the spiritual dimension enter the material world. Under the influence of the material laws of *karma,* the soul, which is by nature eternal, blissful, and full of knowledge, accepts a material body, which must become diseased, grow old, and die. The material world is thus an unsuitable environment for the soul.

The temporary natural beauty of this world, in the form of flowing pure rivers, forests full of trees bearing fruits and flowers, and mountains with cooling waterfalls, is, according to Vedic literature, a reflection of the eternal divine nature of the topmost planet of the spiritual world, known as Goloka Vṛndāvana.

The goal of the Kṛṣṇa consciousness movement is to make this world's nature as much like the divine nature of Goloka Vṛndāvana as possible, and to give everyone the means to return to the spiritual sky at the end of this life. There, in a body free from the contaminations of birth, death, old age, and disease, one can enjoy the transcendentally pure environment of Vṛndāvana in the company of the Lord of Vṛndāvana, Kṛṣṇa, who eternally herds cows called *surabhi* through forests of desire trees.

Bibliography

As It Is newspaper (1980) Volume Two, Number 1. Los Angeles, Bhaktivedanta Book Trust.

Bhaktivedanta Swami Prabhupāda (1972–1980) *Śrīmad-Bhāgavatam of Kṛṣṇa-Dvaipāyana Vyāsa.* Sanskrit text, translation, and commentary. Cantos 1–10 (30 vols.). Los Angeles, Bhaktivedanta Book Trust.

Bhaktivedanta Swami Prabhupada (1974) *Śrī Īśopaniṣad.* Sanskrit text, translation and commentary. Los Angeles, Bhaktivedanta Book Trust.

Bhaktivedanta Swami Prabhupāda (1977) *The Science of Self-Realization.* Los Angeles, Bhaktivedanta Book Trust.

Bhaktivedanta Swami Prabhupāda (1986) *Bhagavad-gītā As It Is.* Sanskrit text, translation, and commentary. London, Bhaktivedanta Book Trust.

Bhaktivedanta Swami Prabhupāda (1987) *Letters from Śrīla Prabhupāda.* Los Angeles, Vaisnava Institute.

Bhaktivedanta Swami Prabhupāda (1988–1991) *Conversations With Śrīla Prabhupāda.* Sandy Ridge, Bhaktivedanta Archives.

Bhaktivedanta Swami Prabhupāda (1990) *The Journey of Self-Discovery.* Los Angeles, Bhaktivedanta Book Trust.

Bohm, David (1957) *Causality and Chance in Modern Physics.* London, Routledge and Kegan Paul.

Bright, Chris (1990) "Shipping Unto Others." *E Magazine,* July–August, pp. 30–35.

Brown, Lester R. (1990) "The Illusion of Progress." In Brown, Lester R., *et al. State of the World: A World Watch Institute Report on Progress Toward a Sustainable Society.* New York, Norton, pp. 1–16.

Brown, Lester R., Flavin, Christopher, and Postel, Sandra (1990) "Picturing a Sustainable Society." In Brown, Lester R., *et al. State of the World: A World Watch Institute Report on Progress Toward a Sustainable Society.* New York, Norton, pp. 171–190.

Caplan, Ruth, and the staff of Environmental Action (1990) *Our Earth, Ourselves.* New York, Bantam.

Carter, Thomas and Lennsen, Nicholas (1990) "Grass Guzzlers." *World Watch* (Letters), January–February, p. 4.

Daley, Herman E. and Cobb, John B., Jr. (1989) *For the Common Good*. Boston, Beacon Press.

Denslow, Julie, and Padoch, Christine (1988) *People of the Tropical Rain Forest*. Berkeley, University of California Press.

Devall, Bill, and Sessions, George (1985) *Deep Ecology*. Layton, Gibbs Smith.

Durning, Alan (1986) "Cost of Beef for Health and Habitat." *Los Angeles Times*, September 21, V3.

Durning, Alan (1990) "How Much Is 'Enough.'" *World Watch*, November–December, pp. 12–19.

Eccles, John C. (1977) "The Brain-Mind Problem as a Frontier of Science." In Robinson, Timothy C. L., ed., *The Future of Science 1975 Nobel Conference*. New York, John Wiley & Sons.

Feinsilber, Mike (1990) "Real Environmentalists Avoid Meat, Doctors Say." Associated Press, *The Gainesville Sun*, April 25, p. 1.

French, Hilary F. (1990a) "A Most Deadly Trade." *World Watch*, July–August, pp. 11–17.

French, Hilary F. (1990b) "Clearing the Air." In Brown, Lester R., *et al. State of the World: A World Watch Institute Report on Progress Toward a Sustainable Society*. New York, Norton, pp. 98–118.

Greenpeace (1990) January–February, p. 20.

Griffin, Donald R. (1984) *Animal Thinking*. Cambridge, Harvard University Press.

Heilbroner, Robert L. (1974) *An Inquiry into the Human Prospect*. New York: W. W. Norton.

Heisenberg, Werner (1971) *Physics and Beyond*. New York, Harper and Row.

Herman, Robin (1990) "Air Pollution Emerges as a World Problem." In Wild, Russell, ed. *The Earth Care Annual*. Emmaus, Rodale Press, pp. 13–16.

Hinrichsen, Don (1988) "Acid Rain and Forest Decline." In Goldsmith, Edward, and Hildyard, Nicholas, *The Earth Report*. Los Angeles, Price Stern Sloan, pp. 65–78.

Huxley, Thomas H. (1892) *Essays on Some Controverted Questions*. London, Macmillan.

Jacobson, Jodi L.(1990) "Holding Back the Sea." In Brown, Lester R., *et al. State of the World: A World Watch Institute Report on Progress Toward a Sustainable Society.* New York, Norton, pp. 79–97.

Lopez, Robert S. (1980) "Wisdom, Science, and Mechanics: The Three Tiers of Medieval Knowledge and the Forbidden Fourth." In Markovits, Andrei S., and Deutsch, Karl W., eds., *Fear of Science—Trust in Science.* Cambridge, Mass.,Oelgeschlager, Gunn & Hain.

Lovelock, Jame E. (1982) *Gaia: A New Look at Life on Earth.* Oxford, Oxford University Press.

Lowe, Marcia D. (1990) "Out of the Car, Into the Future." *World Watch,* November–December, pp. 20–25.

Malthus, Thomas Robert (1803) *On the Principle of Population.* Second edition, reprinted in 1914. New York, Dutton.

Merchant, Carolyn (1980) *The Death of Nature.* Reprinted in 1989 with new preface. San Francisco, Harper and Row.

Mumford, Lewis (1970) *The Myth of the Machine: The Pentagon of Power.* New York, Harcourt Brace Jovanovich.

Nollman, Jim (1990) *Spiritual Ecology.* New York, Bantam.

Pearce, Fred (1990) "Methane: The Hidden Greenhouse Gas." *New Scientist,* May 6, p. 37.

Renner, Michael G. (1989) "Forging Environmental Alliances." *World Watch,* December, pp. 8–15.

Rifkin, Jeremy (1992) *Beyond Beef: The Rise and Fall of the Cattle Culture.* New York, Dutton.

Robbins, John (1989) *Realities 1989, Facts from Diet for a New America, by John Robbins* (brochure).

Roszak, Theodore (1972) *Where the Wasteland Ends.* New York, Doubleday.

Sabom, Michael B. (1982) *Recollections of Death: A Medical Investigation.* New York, Harper and Row.

San Diego Union (1991) "Chernobyl: A tale of lies, ruin, and death." Reprinted from the *Economist* magazine. May 5, p. 5.

Sanger, Margaret (1938) *An Autobiography.* Reprinted 1970 with

preface by Dr. Alan F. Guttmacher, M.D. New York, W. W.
Norton.

Sorokin, Pitirim A. (1964) *The Basic Trends of Our Times.* New
Haven, College & University Press.

Sperry, Roger (1983) "Interview." *Omni,* August.

Stevenson, Ian (1966) *Twenty Cases Suggestive of Reincarnation.*
Richmond, William Byrd Press.

Stevenson, Ian (1974) *Xenoglossy: A Review and Report of a Case.*
Bristol, Wright Publishers.

USA Today (1990) Table. April 17, p. A–4.

Vegetarian Times (1990) "Is a Burger Worth It?" April, pp. 20–21.

World Watch (1990) "Citings." September–October, p. 8.

Notes

Quotations from the works of His Divine Grace A. C. Bhakti-vedanta Swami Prabhupāda (Śrīla Prabhupāda) are from the Bhaktivedanta Book Trust (Los Angeles, Sydney, London) editions of *Bhagavad-gītā As It Is* (1986), *Śrīmad-Bhāgavatam* (1972–1980), *Śrī Īśopaniṣad* (1974), *The Journey of Self-Discovery* (1990), and *The Science of Self-Realization* (1977), and also from the Bhaktivedanta Archives edition of *Conversations with Śrīla Prabhupāda* (1988–1991) and the Vaiṣṇava Institute edition of *Letters From Śrīla Prabhupāda* (1987). In library catalogs, and in this book's bibliography, the author's name is listed as Bhaktivedanta Swami Prabhupāda.

Chapter 1: A Planet in Trouble
1. Nollman 1990, p. 56
2. *Greenpeace* 1990
3. Caplan *et al.* 1990, p. 240
4. *World Watch* 1990
5. Brown 1990, p. 1
6. Durning 1990, p. 17
7. Caplan *et al.* 1990, p. 118
8. French 1990a, pp. 11–12
9. Bright 1990, p. 30
10. Caplan *et al.* 1990, p. 124
11. Caplan *et al.* 1990, p. 215
12. *San Diego Union* 1991
13. Caplan *et al.* 1990, p. 202
14. Lowe 1990, pp. 20–21
15. Durning 1990, p. 16
16. Caplan *et al.* 1990, p. 98
17. Herman 1990, p. 13
18. Brown 1990, p. 14
19. French 1990, p. 109
20. Hinrichsen 1988, p. 69
21. *USA Today* 1990
22. Caplan *et al.* 1990, p. 27
23. Jacobson 1990, p. 80

Chapter 2: Meat and the Environment
1. Rifkin 1992, p. 291
2. Feinsilber 1990
3. Rifkin 1992, pp. 226–227
4. *Vegetarian Times* 1990
5. Denslow and Padoch 1988, p. 168

6. Robbins 1989, p. 2
7. Rifkin 1992, p. 209
8. Durning 1990, p. 16
9. Robbins 1989, p. 1
10. Robbins 1989, p. 1
11. Durning 1986
12. Feinsilber 1990
13. *Vegetarian Times* 1990
14. Daley and Cobb 1989, p. 282
15. Pearce 1990, p. 37
16. Rifkin 1992, p. 226
17. Carter and Lennsen 1990
18. Durning 1986
19. Rifkin 1992, p. 219
20. Feinsilber 1990
21. *Vegetarian Times* 1990
22. Rifkin 1992, pp. 288–289

Chapter 3: Toward a Spiritual Solution
1. Durning 1990, p. 18
2. Durning 1990, p. 12
3. Brown 1990, p. 13
4. Renner 1989, p. 15
5. *Śrīmad-Bhāgavatam* 4.17.25, purport
6. *Śrīmad-Bhāgavatam* 2.2.37, purport
7. Devall and Sessions 1985, pp. 8–9
8. Devall and Sessions 1985, p. 68
9. Devall and Sessions 1985, p. 67

10. Brown *et al.* 1990, p. 190
11. Durning 1990, p. 18
12. Durning 1990, p. 18

Chapter 4: Science, Nature, and the Environment
1. Roszak 1972, p. 135
2. Lopez 1980, p. 19
3. Merchant 1980, p. 169
4. Mumford 1970, p. 117
5. Mumford 1970, p. 40
6. Merchant 1980, p. 30
7. Merchant 1980, p. 63
8. Merchant 1980, p. 66
9. Sorokin 1964, p. 17
10. Sorokin 1964, pp. 17–18
11. Sorokin 1964, p. 25

Chapter 5: A Science of Consciousness
1. Eccles 1977, p. 88
2. Huxley 1892, p. 220
3. Sabom 1982, pp. 162–163
4. Sabom 1982, pp. 183–186
5. Stevenson 1966
6. Stevenson 1974
7. *The Science of Self-Realization*, p. 144

Chapter 6: *Karma* and the Environment
1. Heisenberg 1971, p. 114
2. Sperry 1983, p. 74
3. Heisenberg 1971, p. 114
4. Bohm 1957, p. 133
5. *As It Is* 1980, p. 5.
6. Griffin 1984, p. vi
7. Lovelock 1982, p. vii
8. Lovelock 1982, p. vii
9. *Śrīmad-Bhāgavatam* 3.3.14, purport
10. Sanger 1938, p. 171
11. *Śrīmad-Bhāgavatam* 5.4.9, purport
12. Malthus 1803, p xi

Chapter 7: Rural Communities of ISKCON
1. Heilbroner 1974, p. 139
2. Heilbroner 1974, p. 140
3. Durning 1990, p. 18

Chapter 8: The Environment of the Soul
1. *The Journey of Self Discovery*, pp. 80–81

Resources
A New Way of Living

The following publications and videos provide practical information to help you participate in solving the environmental crisis. ISKCON is the acronym for the International Society for Krishna Consciousness.

Publications on Cow Protection

Ox Power Ki Jaya!

By Paramananda Dasa, ISKCON's Minister of Agriculture for many years. This is a on ox training. Also includes instructions for making basic ox-power equipment. 40 pages; US $5.00 *A $6.95*

Hare Krsna Rural Life

A semiannual newsletter dealing with ox power and other sustainable practices of rural living, as well as the technical and social challenges facing Hare Krsna devotees in rural communities around the world. US $10 per year *A $13.95*

Hinduism and Ecology

By Ranchor Prime, an ISKCON member for more than twenty years. Part of the World Religions and Ecology Series of the World Wide Fund for Nature, this book looks at the environmental values of the Hindu tradition, which underlies the rural communities of ISKCON. 118 pages; $11.95 *A $18.95*

Videos on Cow Protection

Buck and Lou—Get Up!

By the International Society for Cow Protection. This film demonstrates the voice command technique presented in Paramananda's *Ox Power Ki Jaya!* (see above). Other videos are available; please request catalog. 120 minutes; US $20.00 *A $29.95*

Sacred Cow

By ISKCON Television. Learn the true economic, social, and ethical values of cow protection from Vedic experts and agriculturists. 30 minutes; US $12.95 *A $19.95*

Other Videos

Vrindavana, Land of Krsna

Produced by Yadubara Dasa and Visakha Devi, this award-winning film portrays India's sacred town of Vrndavana, which embodies the traditional spiritual way of life reflected in the Krsna consciousness movement's rural communities around the world. By ISKCON Television. 24 minutes; US $12.95 *A $19.95*

Padayatra Worldwide

Join Krishna devotees on the roads of India, the U.S., South America, and Europe as they embark on spiritual adventures of a lifetime. By ISKCON Television. 60 minutes; US $15.00 *A $25.00*

A New Diet

The spiritual, karma-free vegetarian diet of the Krsna consciousness movement is good for the environment as well as the soul.

Cookbooks

Yamuna's Table

By Yamuna Devi, author of the award-winning *Lord Krishna's Cuisine*. This new book combines the rich tradition of India with today's techniques and nutritional concerns. The recipes are adapted to our contemporary taste for low-fat, easily prepared dishes. ISBN 0-525-93487-1, 335 pages; US $23 *A $41.95*

The Best of Lord Krishna's Cuisine

By Yamuna Devi. This book contains 172 of Yamuna's favorite recipes from the only vegetarian cookbook ever selected by the International Association of Culinary Professionals to receive the "Best Cookbook of the Year" award. 242 pages; US $12.99 *A $19.95*

Great Vegetarian Dishes

By Kurma dasa, one of the Hare Krishna movement's most celebrated chefs. Kurma presents hundreds of international recipes in this very practical book. Many full-color photos. ISBN 0-9593659-1-5 192 pages; US $19.99 *A $26.95*

Cooking for Lean Times

By Radha Donna Pessin, with Ayurvedic information by Joseph Sylvester (Bhagavat Das). This book is a practical introduction to informed Ayurvedic cooking. Each recipe includes tips and advice on economy, standard Western nutrition. 160 pages; US $4.99 *A $6.95*

Diet for the 21st Century

By David Wright. A complete guide to egg-free meatless cooking and a karma-free diet. Health, economic, and spiritual advantages to a vegetarian diet; the yoga of cooking and eating. Contains 70 recipes for Italian, Indian, Chinese, Mexican, Middle Eastern, and French dinners. 142 pages; US $6.00 *A $8.50*

Lord Krishna's Cuisine

By Yamuna Devi. International Association of Culinary Professional's "Cookbook of the Year." One of the most exhaustive and authoritative books on Indian cuisine ever published. Over 660 recipes, 330 illustrations. ISBN 0-89647-020-2, 799 pages; US $30 *A $49.95*

The Hare Krishna Book of Vegetarian Cooking

By Adiraja dasa. This publication with many full color illustrations includes explanations about vegetarianism, spices, suggested menus, and culinary aspects of *bhakti-yoga*. 318 pages; US $12.95 *A $19.95*

The Higher Taste

A Contemporary Vedic Library Series Publication. In this introductory guide to gourmet vegetarian cooking and a karma-free diet, one learns why spiritual vegetarianism makes sense physically, economically, ethically, environmentally, and spiritually. 69 recipes; 156 pages; US $2.95 *A $2.65.*

Videos about Vegetarian Cooking & Values

Cooking With Kurma

11 videos, 90–120 minutes each; US $25 *(A $29.95)* each or US $199 *(A $280)* for the set of 11. Cooking is an art, and Kurma is a world-class chef. His recipes are enjoyed in over seventy countries where his best-selling cookbook, *Great Vegetarian Dishes,* has been sold. In this set of videos he teaches in an easy-to-follow manner the art of how to prepare delicious, wholesome vegetarian dishes from around the world.

Volume 1 — Indian Entrees

Scrambled curd, sweet-and-sour mixed vegetables, Gauranga potatoes, and more.

Volume 2 —Indian soups, rice, savories, and chutneys

Creamy yellow pea soup (*dhal*), rice pilaf with nuts and peas, assorted batter-fried vegetables (*pakoras*), tomato chutney, and more.

Volume 3 — Indian breads, drinks, and desserts

Unleavened whole wheat breads (*chapatis*), strawberry yogurt smoothie (*lassi*), classic semolina halavah, vanilla sweet rice, and more.

Volume 4 — East Meets West

Tofu steaks, rainbow brown rice, green bean and broccoli salad, and more.

Volume 5 — Asian Style

Indonesian vegetable stew (*sayur asam*), Thai vegetable curry, Malaysian hot noodles with tofu (*mie goreng*), and more.

Volume 6 — Mediterranean

Italian fried corn bread (*polenta*), Spanish vegetable rice (*paella*), Moroccan couscous with vegetable sauce, and more.

Volume 7 — Indian

Cauliflower and potato supreme, Gujarati yogurt soup (*karhi*), savory whole-meal pancakes (*dosa*), and more.

Volume 8—Mexican-Style Buffet

Mexican baked, stuffed, cheese-filled corn breads (*enchiladas*), Israeli chickpea croquettes (*falafel*), eggplant parmigiana, and more.

Volume 9—Summer Patio Lunch 1

Ricotta-cheese-filled pastries (*calzone*), pasta pesto, *biriyani* vegetable rice casserole, and more.

Volume 10 — Indian Feast

Bengali royal rice (*pushpanna*), Rajasthani spicy dhal-stuffed bread, curried chickpeas, and more.

Volume 11—The Vegetarian Smorgasbord

Potato and pea croquettes, tomato relish, asparagus and tomato quiche, carob fudge cake, steamed cauliflower salad with eggless mayonnaise, and more.

Healthy, Wealthy and Wise
This award-winning video is a great way to introduce your friends to the vegetarian way of life. A well-researched documentary featuring important nutritionists, economists, celebrities, and leading specialists. By ISKCON Television. 30 minutes; US $12.95 *A $19.95*.

Food For Life
A detailed look at the Hare Krishnas' worldwide program of distributing free food. By ISKCON Television. 16 minutes, US $12.95 *A $19.95*

Toward A New Science

The root of our environmental crisis lies in the reductionistic, materialistic worldview of modern science. According to this view, we are biological machines with no higher purpose than exploiting and dominating the earth's resources. A new science based on the proposal that we are irreducible conscious personalities, with our source in an original conscious personality, leads to new values of simple, natural living and spiritual realization.

Publications about Science and Krishna Consciousness

Mechanistic and Nonmechanistic Science
By Richard L. Thompson (Sadaputa dasa).
Holder of a Ph.D. in mathematics, Dr. Thompson shows that the mechanistic paradigm of modern science cannot account for consciousness and the origin of living species. This book includes both popular and technical chapters. 254 pages; US $12.95 *A $19.95*

Vedic Cosmography and Astronomy.
By Richard L. Thompson (Sadaputa dasa).
In this book Dr. Thompson contrasts modern astronomy with Vedic astronomy, especially as it is presented in the Fifth Canto of *Srimad-Bhagavatam*. Many illustrations and tables help to illuminate this difficult subject. 242 pages; US $12.95 *A $19.95*

Consciousness and the Laws of Nature.
By Richard L. Thompson (Sadaputa dasa)
The book includes a historical summary of attempts at describing nature by means of mathematical laws, quantum mechanics, the wave function and its connection to reality, the Heisenberg Uncertainty

principle; the Einstein, Podolsky, Rosen paradox; splitting universes, quantum logic, the fallacy of chance, and higher-order laws. 112 pages; US $9.95 *A $13.95*

Forbidden Archeology

By Michael Cremo (Drutakarma dasa) and Richard L. Thompson (Sadaputa dasa)

The authors present exhaustively researched evidence that directly challenges the commonly held view of when and how *Homo sapiens* appeared on earth. "A remarkably complete review of the scientific evidence concerning human origins," said Dr. Philip E. Johnson, professor at the University of California at Berkeley and the author of *Darwin on Trial.* Hardbound 952 pages; US $40.00 *A $60.00*

Hidden History of the Human Race

A condensed, popular version of *Forbidden Archeology.* Hardbound 322 pages; US $22.95 *A $33.00*

Videos about Science and Krishna Consciousness

Hidden History of the Human Race

By Dr. Richard Thompson (Sadaputa dasa)

Spinning fossils, changing bodies, and digitized picture manipulation. Dr. Thompson has produced ISKCON's first computer-animated science show. Designed for general audiences, this program is guaranteed to create a stir. 30 minutes; US $19.95 *A $29.95*

Simulated Worlds

By Richard Thompson (Sadaputa dasa). As computer technology advances, it is becoming possible to project the consciousness of human subjects into robot bodies moving within computer-simulated environments. Subjects actually experience themselves seeing and moving within a three-dimensional "world" generated by the computer. This video reviews some examples of simulated-worlds technology. It also explores some interesting parallels between the situation of the subject in the simulated world and that of the conditioned self described in Vedic Sankhya philosophy. 45 minutes; US $19.95 *A $29.95*

Sources of Nonmaterial Happiness

According to the *Vedanta-sutra*, the soul is naturally illuminated by transcendental happiness. By experiencing this higher happiness, one can rise above the materialistic desires fueling the industrial production that has brought the world to the point of environmental catastrophe. The natural spiritual happiness of the soul can be awakened by the practice of *bhakti-yoga*, the *yoga* of devotion, which is practiced in the centers of the International Society for Krishna Consciousness.

Books Explaining Bhakti-yoga

The following books are by His Divine Grace A.C. Bhaktivedanta Swami Prabhupada, founder-*acarya* of the International Society for Krishna Consciousness.

Bhagavad-gita As It Is

The *Bhagavad-gita* is universally renowned as the jewel of India's spiritual wisdom. Spoken by Lord Krsna to His intimate devotee Arjuna, the *Gita's* seven hundred concise verses provide a definitive guide to self-realization, yoga, karma, and man's relationship with his environment and, ultimately, with God. 1,047 pages; US $26.95 A $33.95

Srimad-Bhagavatam

The complete science of *bhakti-yoga*. Srila Prabhupada writes in his preface: "Human society, at the present moment, is not in the darkness of oblivion. It has made rapid progress in the field of material comforts, education and economic development throughout the entire world. But there is a pinprick somewhere in the social body at large, and therefore there are large-scale quarrels, even over less important issues. There is need of a clue as to how humanity can become one in peace, friendship, and prosperity with a common cause. *Srimad-Bhagavatam* will fill this need, for it is a cultural presentation for the respiritualization of the entire human society."

Careful study of *Srimad-Bhagavatam* elevates one beyond material distress and duality, provides clear knowledge of material and spiritual realities, and yields the ultimate perfection, love of God, or Krishna consciousness. 18 volumes; US $360 A $500

Order Form

Make check or money order payable to Bhaktivedanta Book Trust and send to:

The Bhaktivedanta Book Trust
3764 Watseka Avenue Dept. DN-Mass
Los Angeles, CA 90034

In Australia contact The Bhaktivedanta Book Trust at (02) 666-6466
Other countries contact your local ISKCON Center (see address list)

Name _____
<small>Please Print</small>

Address _____

City _____ ST _____ Zip _____

Description	Qty.	Price	Total

Subtotal US $ _____

CA Sales Tax 8.25% US $ _____

Shipping 15% of Subtotal US $ _____

TOTAL US $ _____

Index

The International Society for Krishna Consciousness
Founder-Acarya: His Divine Grace A. C. Bhaktivedanta Swami Prabhupada

Centers Around the World

♦ Temples with restaurants or dining.

NORTH AMERICA

CANADA
Calgary, Alberta — 313 Fourth St. N.E., T2E 3S3/ Tel. (403) 238-0602
Montreal, Quebec — 1626 Pie IX Boulevard, H1V 2C5/ Tel. (514) 521-1301
♦ **Ottawa, Ontario** — 212 Somerset St. E., K1N 6V4/ Tel. (613) 565-6544
Regina, Saskatchewan — 1279 Retallack St., S4T 2H8/ Tel. (306) 525-1640
♦ **Toronto, Ontario** — 243 Avenue Rd., M5R 2J6/ Tel. (416) 922-5415
♦ **Vancouver, B.C.** — 5462 S.E. Marine Dr., Burnaby V5J 3G8/ Tel. (604) 433-9728
Victoria, B.C. —1505 Arrow Rd., V8N 1C3/ Tel. (604) 721-2102

FARM COMMUNITY
Ashcroft, B.C. — Saranagati Dhama, Box 99, V0K 1A0

ADDITIONAL RESTAURANTS
Hamilton, Ontario — Govinda's, 195 Locke St. South, L8T 4B5/ Tel. (416) 523-6209
Vancouver — The Hare Krishna Place, 46 Begbie St., New Westminster

U.S.A.
♦ **Atlanta, Georgia** — 1287 South Ponce de Leon Ave. N.E., 30306/ Tel. (404) 378-9234
Baltimore, Maryland — 200 Bloomsbury Ave., Catonsville, 21228/ Tel. (410) 744-1624 or 4069
Boise, Idaho — 1615 Martha St., 83706/ Tel. (208) 344-4274
Boston, Massachusetts — 72 Commonwealth Ave., 02116/ Tel. (617) 247-8611
Champaign, Illinois — 608 W. Elm St., 61801/ Tel. (217) 344-2562
♦ **Chicago, Illinois** — 1716 W. Lunt Ave., 60626/ Tel. (312) 973-0900
Columbus, Ohio — 379 W. Eighth Ave., 43201/ Tel. (614) 421-1661
♦ **Dallas, Texas** — 5430 Gurley Ave., 75223/ Tel. (214) 827-6330
♦ **Denver, Colorado** — 1400 Cherry St., 80220/ Tel. (303) 333-5461
♦ **Detroit, Michigan** — 383 Lenox Ave., 48215/ Tel. (313) 824-6000
Encinitas, California — 468 First St., 92024/ Tel. (619) 634-1698

Gainesville, Florida — 214 N.W. 14th St., 32603/ Tel. (904) 336-4183
Gurabo, Puerto Rico — Route 181, P.O. Box 8440 HC-01, 00778-9763/ Tel. (809) 737-1658
Hartford, Connecticut — 1683 Main St., E. Hartford, 06108/ Tel. (203) 289-7252
♦ **Honolulu, Hawaii** — 51 Coelho Way, 96817/ Tel. (808) 595-3947
Houston, Texas — 1320 W. 34th St., 77018/ Tel. (713) 686-4482
♦ **Laguna Beach, California** — 285 Legion St., 92651/ Tel. (714) 494-7029
Long Island, New York — 197 S. Ocean Ave., Freeport, 11520/ Tel. (516) 867-9045
♦ **Los Angeles, California** — 3764 Watseka Ave., 90034/ Tel. (310) 836-2676
♦ **Miami, Florida** — 3220 Virginia St., 33133 (mail: P.O. Box 337, Coconut Grove, FL 33233)/ Tel. (305) 442-7218
♦ **New Orleans, Louisiana** — 2936 Esplanade Ave., 70119/ Tel. (504) 586-9379
New York, New York — 305 Schermerhorn St., Brooklyn, 11217/ Tel. (718) 855-6714
New York, New York — 26 Second Avenue, 10003/ Tel. (212) 420-8803
Philadelphia, Pennsylvania — 41 West Allens Lane, 19119/ Tel. (215) 247-4600
Portland, Oregon — 5137 N.E. 42 Ave., 97218/ Tel. (503) 234-8971
♦ **St. Louis, Missouri** — 3926 Lindell Blvd., 63108/ Tel. (314) 535-8085
San Diego, California — 1030 Grand Ave., Pacific Beach, 92109/ Tel. (619) 483-2500
San Francisco, California — 84 Carl St., 94117/ Tel. (415) 661-7320
♦ **San Francisco, California** — 2334 Stuart St., Berkeley, 94705/Tel. (510) 540-9215
Seattle, Washington — 1420 228th Ave. S.E., Issaquah, 98027/ Tel. (206) 391-3293
Spanish Fork, Utah — KHQN Radio, 8628 South State St., 84660/ Tel. (801) 798-3559
Tallahassee, Florida — 1323 Nylic St. (mail: P.O. Box 20224, 32304)/ Tel. (904) 681-9258
Topanga, California — 20395 Callon Dr., 90290/ Tel. (213) 455-1658
Towaco, New Jersey — P.O. Box 109, 07082/ Tel. (201) 299-0970
♦ **Tucson, Arizona** — 711 E. Blacklidge Dr., 85719/ Tel. (602) 792-0630

Walla Walla, Washington — 314 E. Poplar, 99362/ Tel. (509) 525-7133

Washington, D.C. — 600 Ninth St, NE, 20002/ Tel. (202) 547-1444

Washington, D.C. — 10310 Oaklyn Dr., Potomac, Maryland 20854/ Tel. (301) 299-2100

FARM COMMUNITIES

Alachua, Florida (New Ramana-reti) — Box 819, 32615/ Tel. (904) 462-2017

Carriere, Mississippi (New Talavan) — 31492 Anner Road, 39426/ Tel. (601) 799-1354

Gurabo, Puerto Rico (New Govardhana Hill) — (contact ISKCON Gurabo)

Hillsborough, North Carolina (New Goloka) — 1032 Dimmocks Mill Rd., 27278/ Tel. (919) 732-6492

Mulberry, Tennessee (Murari-sevaka) — Rt. No. 1, Box 146-A, 37359/ Tel (615) 759-6888

Port Royal, Pennsylvania (Gita Nagari) — R.D. No. 1, Box 839, 17082/ Tel. (717) 527-4101

ADDITIONAL RESTAURANTS AND DINING

Boise, Idaho — Govinda's, 500 W. Main St., 83702/ Tel. (208) 338-9710

Eugene, Oregon — Govinda's Vegetarian Buffet, 270 W. 8th St., 97401/ Tel. (503) 686-3531

Gainesville, Florida — Radha's, 125 NW 23rd Ave., 32609/ Tel. (904) 376-9012

Gurabo, Puerto Rico — 1 (809) 737-7039

EUROPE

UNITED KINGDOM AND IRELAND

Belfast, Northern Ireland — 140 Upper Dunmurray Lane, BT17 OHE/ Tel. +44 (01232) 620530

Birmingham, England — 84 Stanmore Rd., Edgebaston, B16 9TB/ Tel. +44 (0121) 420-4999

Bristol, England — 48 Station Rd., Nailsea, Bristol BS19 2PB/ Tel. +44 (01275) 853788

Coventry, England — Sri Sri Radha Krishna Cultural Centre, Kingfield Rd., Radford (mail: 19 Gloucester St., CV1 3BZ)/ Tel. +44 (01203) 555420

Dublin, Ireland — 56 Dame St., Dublin 2/ Tel. +353 (01) 679-1306

Glasgow, Scotland — Karuna Bhavan, Bankhouse Rd., Lesmahagow, Lanarkshire ML11 0ES/ Tel. +44 (01555) 894790

Leicester, England — 21/21A Thoresby St., North Evington, Leicester LE5 4GU/ Tel. +44 (01533) 762587

Liverpool, England — 114A Bold St., Liverpool L1 4HY/ Tel. +44 (0151) 708 9400

♦ **London, England (city)** — 10 Soho St., London W1V 5DA/ Tel. +44 (0171) 4373662 (business hours), 4393606 (other times); Govinda's Restaurant: 4374928

London, England (country) — Bhaktivedanta Manor, Letchmore Heath, Watford, Hertfordshire WD2 8EP/ Tel. +44 (01923) 857244

London, England (south) — 42 Enmore Road, South Norwood, London SE25/ Tel. +44 (0181) 656-4296

Manchester, England — 20 Mayfield Rd., Whalley Range, Manchester M16 8FT/ Tel. +44 (0161) 2264416

Newcastle upon Tyne, England — 21 Leazes Park Rd., NE1 4PF/ Tel. +44 (0191) 2220150

FARM COMMUNITIES

County Wicklow, Ireland — Rathgorragh, Kiltegan/ Tel. +353 508-73305

Lisnaskea, North Ireland — Hare Krishna Island, BT92 9GN Lisnaskea, Co. Fremanagh/ Tel. +44 (03657) 21512

London, England — (contact Bhaktivedanta Manor)

(Krishna conscious programs are held regularly in more than twenty other cities in the U.K. For information, contact Bhaktivedanta Books Ltd., Reader Services Dept., P.O. Box 324, Borehamwood, Herts WD6 1NB/ Tel. +44 [0181] 905-1244.)

CROATIA

Cakovec — Radnicka 2, Savska Ves, 42300 Cakovec/ Tel. +385 (042) 311 195

Osijek — Bartola Kasica 32, 54000 Osijek/ Tel. +385 (054) 127 829

Pula — Vinkuran centar 58, 52000 Pula/ Tel. +385 (052) 541 425, mobitel 484 279

Rijeka — BKC, p.p. 61, 51000 Rijeka/ Tel. +385 (051) 335893

Split — Mutogras 20, 58312 Podstrana, Split/ Tel. +385 (021) 651 265

Zagreb — ISKCON vedske studije, I Bizek 5, 41090 Zagreb (mail: CVS, p.p. 68, 41001 Zagreb)/ Tel. & Fax +385 (01) 190548

GERMANY

♦ **Berlin** — Bhakti Yoga Center, Muskauer Str. 27, 10997 Berlin/ Tel. +49 (030) 618 9112

Flensburg — Neuhoerup 1, 24980 Hoerup/ Tel. +49 (04639) 73 36

Hamburg — Muehlenstr. 93, 25421 Pinneberg/ Tel. +49 (04101) 2 39 31

◆ **Heidelberg** — Center for Vedic Studies, Kürfuersten-Anlage 5, 69115 Heidelberg (mail: P.O. Box 101726, 69007 Heidelberg)/ Tel. +49 (06221) 16 51 01

◆ **Köln** — Taunusstr. 40, 51105 Köln/ Tel. +49 (0221) 830 37 78

Munich — Tal 38, 80331 Munchen/ Tel +49 (089) 29 23 17

Nuremberg — Bhakti Yoga Center, Kopernikusplatz 12, 90459 Nürnberg/ Tel. +49 (0911) 45 32 86

Weimar — Rothauserbergweg 6, 99425 Weimar/ Tel. +49 (03643) 5 95 48

Wiesbaden — Schiersteiner Strasse 6, 65187 Wiesbaden/ Tel. +49 (0611) 37 33 12

FARM COMMUNITY

Jandelsbrunn — Nava Jiyada Nrsimha Ksetra, Zielberg 20, 94118 Jandelsbrunn/ Tel +49 (08583) 316

ADDITIONAL RESTAURANT

Berlin — Higher Taste, Kurfuerstendamm 157/158, 10709 Berlin/ Tel. +49 (030) 892 99 17

ITALY

Asti — Roatto, Frazione Valle Reale 20/ Tel. +39 (0141) 938406

Bergamo — Villaggio Hare Krishna, Via Galileo Galilei 41, 24040 Chignolo D'isola (BG)/ Tel. +39 (035) 490706

Bologna — Via Ramo Barchetta 2. 40010 Bentivoglio (BO)/ Tel. +39 (051) 863924

◆ **Catania** — Via San Nicolo al Borgo 28, 95128 Catania, Sicily/ jTel. +39 (095) 522-252

Naples — Via Vesuvio, N33, Ercolano LNA7/ Tel. +39 (081) 739-0398

Rome — Nepi, Sri Gaura Mandala, Via Mazzanese Km. 0,700 (dalla Cassia uscita Calcata), Pian del Pavone (Viterbo)/ Tel. +39 (0761) 527038

Vicenza — Via Roma 9, 36020 Albettone (Vicenza)/ Tel. +39 (0444) 790573 or 790566

FARM COMMUNITY

Florence (Villa Vrindavan) — Via Communale degli Scopeti 108, S. Andrea in Percussina, San Casciano, Val di Pesa (FI) 5002/ Tel. +39 (055) 820-054

ADDITIONAL RESTAURANT

Milan — Govinda's, Via Valpetrosa 3/5, 20123 Milano / Tel. +39 (02) 862-417

POLAND

◆ **Gdansk** — ul. Cedrowa 5, Gdansk 80-125 (mail: MTSK 80-958 Gdansk 50 skr. poczt. 364)/ Tel. +48 (58) 329665

Kracow — ISKCON, ul. Ehrenberga 15, 31-309 Krakow/ Tel. +48 (12) 36 28 85

Poznan — ul. Nizinna 26, 61-424 Poznan/ Tel. & Fax +48 (61) 323838

Warsaw — Mysiadlo k. Warszawy, ul. Zakret 11, 05-500 Piaseczno / Tel. +48 (22)562-711

Wroclaw — ul. Nowowiejska 87/8, 50-340 Wroclaw/ Tel. & Fax +48 (71) 225704

FARM COMMUNITY

New Santipura — Czarnow 21, k. Kamiennej gory, woj. Jelenia gora/ Tel. +48 8745-1892

SWEDEN

Gothenburg — Höjdgätan 22, 431 36 Moelndal/ Tel. +46 (031) 879648

◆ **Grödinge** — Korsnäs Gård, 14792 Grödinge/ Tel. +46 (0500) 29151

Karlstad — ISKCON, Box 5155, 650 05 Karlstadø

◆ **Lund** — Bredg 28 ipg, 222 21/ Tel. +46 (046) 120413

Malmö — Hare Krishna Temple, Gustav Adolfs Torg 10 A, 211 39 Malmö/ Tel. +46 (040) 127181

◆ **Stockholm** — Fridhemsgatan 22, 11240 Stockholm/ Tel. +46 (08) 6549 002

◆ **Uppsala** — Nannaskolan sal F 3, Kungsgatan 22 (mail: Box 833, 751 08, Uppsala)/ Tel. +46 (018) 102924 or 509956

FARM COMMUNITY

Järna — Almviks Gård, 153 95 Järna/ Tel. +46 (8551) 52050; 52105

ADDITIONAL RESTAURANTS

Göthenburg — Govinda's, Storgatan 20,S-411 38 Göthenburg / Tel. +46 (031) 139698

Malmö — Higher Taste, Amiralsgatan 6, S-211 55 Malmö/ Tel. +46 (040) 970600

Stockholm — Gopal, Timmermansgatan 13, 117 25 Stockholm/ Tel. +46 (08) 6441035

SWITZERLAND

Basel — Hammerstrasse 11, 4058 Basel/ Tel. +41 (061) 693 26 38

Bern — Marktgasse 7, 3011 Bern/ Tel. +41 (031) 312 38 25

Lugano — Via ai Grotti, 6862 Rancate (TI)/ Tel. +41 (091) 46 66 16

Zürich — Bergstrasse 54, 8030 Zürich/ Tel. +41 (1) 262-33-88

Oslo, Norway — Krishna's Cuisine, Kirkeveien 59B, 0364 Oslo/ Tel. +47 22606250
Vienna, Austria — Govinda, Lindengasse 2A, 1070 Vienna/ Tel. +43 (01) 5222817

COMMONWEALTH OF INDEPENDENT STATES
RUSSIA
Moscow — Khoroshevskoye shosse d.8, korp.3, 125 284, Moscow/ Tel. +7 (095) 255-67-11
Nijni Novgorod — ul. Ivana Mochalova, 7-69, 603904 Nijni Novgorod/ Tel. +7 (8312) 252592
Novosibirsk — ul. Leningradskaya 111-20, Novosibirsk
Perm (Ural Region) — Pr. Mira, 113–142, 614065 Perm/ Tel. +7 (3442) 335740
St. Petersburg — ul. Burtseva 20-147, St. Petersburg 190000/ Tel. +7 (0812) 150-28-80
Ulyanovsk — ul Glinki, 10 /Tel. +7 (0842) 221-42-89
Vladivostok — ul. Ridneva 5–1, 690087 Vladivostok/ Tel. +7 (4232) 268943

ADDITIONAL RESTAURANTS
Arkhangelsk—Tel. (8182) 46-78-48
Novgorod—ul. Kosmonavtov 18/1 / Tel. (81600) 22-642
Rostov-na-don—Tel. (8932) 51-04-56
St. Petersburg—Govinda, Prospekt Maklina, 58 (812) 113-78-96
Sochi—Bitha, ul. Lesnaya, 81a
Vladikavkaz—ul. Kostahetagurova, 50
Vladivostok—Gopala, Tel. (4232) 26-89-43,
Yekaterinburg—Sankirtana Ul. Bardina, 23/ Tel. (3432) 48-43-51

UKRAINE
Chernigov — ul. Krasnogvardeyskaya, 10-56, 250033 Chernigov
Dnepropetrovsk — ul. Ispolkomovskaya, 56A, 320029 Dnepropetrovsk/ Tel. +7 (0562) 445029
Donetsk — ul. Treneva, 3-44, Donetsk
Kharkov — ul. Verhne-Gievskaya, 43, 310015 Kharkov
Kiev — ul. Menjinskogo, 21-B., 252054 Kiev/Tel.+7 (044) 2444944
Lvov — 292066 Lvivska obl. Buski rajon. S. Zbolotni Chuchmani
Nikolayev — Sudostroitelny pereulok, 5/8, Nikolayev 377052
Odessa — Klubnichny Per., Vinogradny Tupik, Sanatory "Rodina," 8 Kor.
Vinnitza — ul. Chkalov St., 5, Vinnitza 26800/ Tel. +7 (04322) 23152

OTHER COUNTRIES
♦ **Alma Ata, Kazakstan** — Per Kommunarov, 5, 480022 Alma Ata/ Tel. +7 (3272) 35-14-44
Baku, Azerbaijan — Pos. 8-i km, per. Sardobi 2, Baku 370060/ Tel. +7 (8922) 212376
Bishkek, Kyrgizstan — Per. Omski, 5, 720000 Bishkek/ Tel. +7 (3312) 472683
Dushanbe, Tadjikistan — ul Anzob, 38, 724001 Dushanbe/ Tel. +7 (3772) 271830
Kishinev, Moldova — ul. George Asaki, 68/1-105, 277028 Kishinev/ Tel. +7 (0127) 73-70-24
Minsk, Belarus — ul. Pavlova 11, 220 053 Minsk
Sukhumi, Georgia — Pr. Mira 274, Sukhumi
Tbilisi, Georgia — ul. Kacharava, 16, 380044 Tbilisi/ Tel. +7 (8832) 623326
Yerevan, Armenia — ul. Krupskoy 18, 375019 Yerevan/ Tel. +7 (8852) 275106

AUSTRALASIA

AUSTRALIA
Adelaide — 227 Henley Beach Rd., Torrensville, S. A. 5031/ Tel. +61 (08) 234-1378
Brisbane — 95 Bank Rd., Graceville, Q.L.D. (mail: P.O. Box 83, Indooroopilly 4068)/ Tel. +61 (07) 379-5455

Canberra — P.O Box 1411, Canberra ACT 2060/ Tel. +61 (06) 290-1869
Melbourne — 197 Danks St., Albert Park, Victoria 3206 (mail: P.O. Box 125)/ Tel. +61 (03) 699-5122
Perth — 356 Murray St., Perth (mail: P.O. Box 102, Bayswater, W. A. 6053)/ Tel. +61 (09) 481-1114 or 370-1552 (evenings)
♦ **Sydney** — 180 Falcon St., North Sydney, N.S.W. 2060 (mail: P. O. Box 459, Cammeray, N.S.W. 2062)/ Tel. +61 (02) 959-4558
♦ **Sydney** — 3296 King St., Newtown 2042/ Tel. +61 (02) 550-6524

FARM COMMUNITIES
Bambra (New Nandagram) — Oak Hill, Dean's Marsh Rd., Bambra, VIC 3241/ Tel. +61 (052) 88-7383
Millfield, N.S.W. — New Gokula Farm, Lewis Lane (off Mt.View Rd. Millfield near Cessnock), N.S.W. (mail: P.O. Box 399, Cessnock 2325, N.S.W.)/ Tel. +61 (049) 98-1800

Murwillumbah (New Govardhana) — Tyalgum Rd., Eungella, via Murwillumbah N. S. W. 2484 (mail: P.O. Box 687)/ Tel. +61 (066) 72-6579

ADDITIONAL RESTAURANTS

Brisbane — Govinda's, 1st floor, 99 Elizabeth Street/ Tel. +61 (07) 210-0255
Melbourne — Crossways, Floor 1, 123 Swanston St., Melbourne, Victoria 3000/ Tel. +61 (03) 650-2939
Melbourne — Gopal's, 139 Swanston St., Melbourne, Victoria 3000/ Tel. +61 (03) 650-1578
Murwillumbah—91 Main Street, Murwillumbah, NSW 2484/ Tel. +61 (66) 726767
Perth — Hare Krishna Food for Life, 200 William St., Northbridge, WA 6003/ Tel. +61 (09) 227-1684
Sydney — Govinda's Upstairs, 112 Darlinghurst Rd., Darlinghurst, N.S.W. 2010/ Tel. +61 (02) 380-5162

NEW ZEALAND, FIJI, AND PAPUA NEW GUINEA

Christchurch, New Zealand — 83 Bealey Ave. (mail: P.O. Box 25-190 Christchurch)/ Tel. +64 (03) 3665-174
Labasa, Fiji — Delailabasa (mail: P.O. Box 133)/ Tel. +679 812912
Lautoka, Fiji — 5 Tavewa Ave. (mail: P.O. Box 125)/ Tel. +679 664112
Port Moresby, Papua New Guinea — Section 23, Lot 46, Gordonia St., Hohola (mail: P. O. Box 571, POM NCD)/ Tel. +675 259213
Rakiraki, Fiji — Rewasa, Rakiraki (mail: P.O. Box 204)/ Tel. +679 694243
Suva, Fiji — Nasinu 7½ miles (mail: P.O. Box 7315)/ Tel. +679 393599
Wellington, New Zealand — 60 Wade St., Wadestown, Wellington (mail: P.O. Box 2753, Wellington)/ Tel. +64 (04) 4720510

FARM COMMUNITY

Auckland, New Zealand (New Varshan) — Hwy. 18, Riverhead, next to Huapai Golf Course (mail: R.D. 2, Kumeu, Auckland)/ Tel. +64 (09) 4128075

RESTAURANTS

Auckland, New Zealand — Gopal's, Civic House (1st floor), 291 Queen St./ Tel. +64 (09) 3034885
Christchurch, New Zealand — Gopal's, 143 Worcester St./ Tel. +64 (03) 3667-035
Labasa, Fiji — Hare Krishna Restaurant, Naseakula Road/ Tel. +679 811364

Lautoka, Fiji — Gopal's, Corner of Yasawa St. and Naviti St./ Tel. +679 662990
Suva, Fiji — Gopal's, 18 Pratt St./ Tel. +679 314154

AFRICA

NIGERIA

Abeokuta — Ibadan Rd., Obanatoka (mail: P.O. Box 5177)
Benin City — 108 Lagos Rd., Uselu/ Tel. +234 (052) 247900
Enugu — 8 Church Close, off College Rd., Housing Estate, Abakpa-Nike
Ibadan — 1 Ayo Akintoba St., Agbowo, University of Ibadan
Jos — 5A Liberty Dam Close, P.O. Box 6557, Jos
Kaduna — 8B Dabo Rd., Kaduna South, P.O. Box 1121, Kaduna
Lagos — 25 Jaiyeola Ajata St., Ajao Estate, off International Airport Express Rd., Lagos (mail: P.O. Box 0799)/ Tel. & Fax +234 (01) 876169
Port Harcourt — Second Tarred Road, Ogwaja Waterside (mail: P.O. Box 4429, Trans Amadi)
Warri — Okwodiete Village, Kilo 8, Effurun/ Orerokpe Rd. (mail: P.O. Box 1922, Warri)

SOUTH AFRICA

Cape Town — 17 St. Andrews Rd., Rondebosch 7700/ Tel. +27 (021) 689-1529
♦ **Durban** — Chatsworth Centre, Chatsworth 4030 (mail: P.O. Box 56003)/ Tel. +27 (31) 433-328
♦ **Johannesburg** — 14 Goldreich St., Hillbrow 2001 (mail: P.O. Box 10667, Johannesburg 2000)/ Tel. +27 (011) 484-3273
Port Elizabeth — 15 Whitehall Court, Western Rd., Central Port Elizabeth 6001/ Tel. & Fax +27 (41) 521-102

OTHER COUNTRIES

Kampala, Uganda — Bombo Rd., near Makerere University (mail: P.O. Box 1647, Kampala)
Kisumu, Kenya — P.O. Box 547/ Tel. +254 (035) 42546
Marondera, Zimbabwe — 6 Pine Street (mail: P.O. Box 339)/ Tel. +263 (028) 8877801
Mombasa, Kenya — Hare Krishna House, Sauti Ya Kenya and Kisumu Rds. (mail: P.O. Box 82224, Mombasa)/ Tel. +254 (011) 312248

Nairobi, Kenya — Muhuroni Close, off West Nagara Rd. (mail: P.O. Box 28946, Nairobi)/ Tel. +254 (02) 744365

Phoenix, Mauritius — Hare Krishna Land, Pont Fer, Phoenix (mail: P. O. Box 108, Quartre Bornes, Mauritius)/ Tel. +230 696-5804

FARM COMMUNITY

Mauritius (ISKCON Vedic Farm) — Hare Krishna Rd., Vrindaban, Bon Acceuil/ Tel. +230 418-3955

ASIA

INDIA

Agartala, Tripura — Assam-Agartala Rd., Banamalipur, 799001

Ahmedabad, Gujarat — Sattelite Rd., Gandhinagar Highway Crossing, Ahmedabad 380054/
Tel. (079) 649945 or 649982

Allahabad, U. P. — 403 Baghambari Housing Scheme, Bharadwaj Puram, Allahapur, Allahabad 211006/ Tel. (0532) 609213 or 607885

Bamanbore, Gujarat — N.H. 8A, Surendra-nagar District

Bangalore, Karnataka — Hare Krishna Hill, 1 'R' Block, Chord Road, Rajaji Nagar 560010/ Tel. (080) 321956 or 342818 or 322346

Bhayandar, Maharashtra — Shivaji Chowk, Station Rd., Bhayandar (West), Thane 401101/ Tel. (022) 8191920

◆ **Bhubaneswar, Orissa** — National Highway No. 5, Nayapali, 751001/ Tel. (0674) 413517 or 413475

◆ **Bombay, Maharashtra** — Hare Krishna Land, Juhu 400 049/ Tel. (022) 6206860

Bombay, Maharashtra — 7 K. M. Munshi Marg, Chowpatty, 400007/ Tel. (022) 3634078

Belgaum, Karnataka — Shukravar Peth, Tilak Wadi, 590006

Calcutta, W. Bengal — 3C Albert Rd., 700017/ Tel. (033) 2473757 or 2476075

Chandigarh — Hare Krishna Land, Dakshin Marg, Sector 36-B, 160036/ Tel. (0172) 601590 and 603232

Coimbatore, Tamil Nadu — 387, VGR Puram, Dr. Alagesan Rd., 641011/ Tel. (0422) 445978 or 442749

Gauhati, Assam — Ulubari Charali, Gauhati 781001/ Tel. (0361) 31208

Guntur, A.P. — Opp. Sivalayam, Peda Kakani 522509

Hanumkonda, A.P. — Neeladri Rd., Kapuwada, 506011/ Tel. 08712-77399

Hyderabad, A.P. — Hare Krishna Land, Nampally Station Rd., 500001/ Tel. (040) 592018 or 552924

Imphal, Manipur — Hare Krishna Land, Airport Road, 795001/ Tel. (0385) 21587

Kollur, Karnataka—Garuda Guha Ashram, Kollur 576220/ Tel. (8254) 58211

Kurukshetra, Haryana — 369 Gudri Muhalla, Main Bazaar, 132118/ Tel. (1744) 32806 or 33529

Madras, Tamil Nadu — 59, Burkit Rd., T. Nagar, 600017/ Tel. 443266

Mangalore, Karnataka — New Bungalow, D. No. 22-3-524, near Morgans Gate, Jeppu, Mangalore (mail: P.O. Box 15, Mangalore 575001)/ Tel. (824) 28895

◆ **Mayapur, W. Bengal** — Shree Mayapur Chandrodaya Mandir, Shree Mayapur Dham, Dist. Nadia (mail: P.O. Box 10279, Ballyganj, Calcutta 700019)/ Tel. (03472) 45250

Moirang, Manipur — Nongban Ingkhon, Tidim Rd./ Tel. 795133

Nagpur, Maharashtra — 70 Hill Road, Ramnagar, 440010/ Tel. (0712) 529932

New Delhi — Sant Nagar Main Road (Garhi), behind Nehru Place Complex (mail: P. O. Box 7061), 110065/ Tel. (011) 6419701 or 6412058

New Delhi — 14/63, Punjabi Bagh, 110026/ Tel. (011) 5410782

Pandharpur, Maharashtra — Hare Krsna Ashram (across Chandrabhaga River), Dist. Sholapur, 413304/ Tel. (0218) 623473

Patna, Bihar — Rajendra Nagar Road No. 12, 800016/ Tel. (0612) 50765

Pune, Maharashtra — 4 Tarapoor Rd., Camp, 411001/ Tel. (0212) 667259

Puri, Orissa — Sipasurubuli Puri, Dist. Puri

Puri, Orissa — Bhakti Kuthi, Swargadwar, Puri/ Tel. (06752) 23740

Secunderabad, A.P. — 27 St. John's Road, 500026/ Tel. (040) 805232

Silchar, Assam — Ambikapatti, Silchar, Cachar Dist., 788004

Siliguri, W. Bengal — Gitalpara, 734401/ Tel. (0353) 26619

Surat, Gujarat — Rander Rd., Jahangirpura, 395005/ Tel. (0261) 685516 or 685891

Tirupati, A. P. — K.T. Road, Vinayaka Nagar, 517507/ Tel. (08574) 20114

Trivandrum, Kerala — T.C. 224/1485, WC Hospital Rd., Thycaud, 695014/ Tel. (0471) 68197

Udhampur, Jammu and Kashmir — Srila Prabhupada Ashram, Prabhupada Marg, Prabhupada Nagar, Udhampur 182101/ Tel. (0199) 298

Vadodara, Gujarat — Hare Krishna Land, Gotri Rd., 390021/ Tel. (0265) 326299 or 321012

Vallabh Vidyanagar, Gujarat — ISKCON Hare Krishna Land, 338120/ Tel. (02692) 30796

♦ **Vrindavana, U. P.** — Krishna-Balaram Mandir, Bhaktivedanta Swami Marg, Raman Reti, Mathura Dist., 281124/ Tel. (0565) 442-478 or 442-355

FARM COMMUNITIES

Ahmedabad District, Gujarat — Hare Krishna Farm, Katwada (contact ISKCON Ahmedabad)

Assam — Karnamadhu, Dist. Karimganj

Chamorshi, Maharashtra — 78 Krishnanagar Dham, District Gadhachiroli, 442603

Hyderabad, A. P. — P. O. Dabilpur Village, Medchal Tq., R.R. District, 501401/ Tel. 552924

Mayapur, West Bengal — (contact ISKCON Mayapur)

Shimoga Dist., Karnataka—Vallor Valley, P.O. Nagodi, Hosanagar Taluq 577425, Shimoga Dist., Karnataka

ADDITIONAL RESTAURANT

Calcutta — Hare Krishna Karma-Free Confectionary, 6 Russel Street, Calcutta 700071

OTHER COUNTRIES

Bali, Indonesia — (Contact ISKCON Jakarta)

Bangkok, Thailand — 139 Soi Puttha Osotha, New Road (near GPO), Bangkok 10500/ Tel. +66 (02) 234-1006

Cagayan de Oro, Philippines — 30 Dahlia St., Ilaya Carmen, 900 (c/o Sepulveda's Compound)

Chittagong, Bangladesh — Caitanya Cultural Society, Sri Pundarik Dham, Mekhala, Hathzari (mail: GPO Box 877, Chittagong)/ Tel. +88 (031) 225822

Colombo, Sri Lanka — 188 New Chetty St., Colombo 13/ Tel. +94 (01) 433325

Dhaka, Bangladesh — 5 Chandra Mohon Basak St., Banagram, Dhaka 1203/ Tel. +880 (02) 252428

♦ **Hong Kong** — 27 Chatam Road South, 6/F, Kowloon/ Tel. +852 7396818

Iloilo City, Philippines — 13-1-1 Tereos St., La Paz, Iloilo City, Iloilo/ Tel. +63 (033) 73391

Jakarta, Indonesia — P.O. Box 2694, Jakarta Pusat 10001/ Tel. +62 (021) 4899646

Jessore, Bangladesh — Nitai Gaur Mandir, Kathakhali Bazaar, P. O. Panjia, Dist. Jessore

Jessore, Bangladesh — Rupa-Sanatana Smriti Tirtha, Ramsara, P. O. Magura Hat, Dist. Jessore

Kathmandu, Nepal — Budhanilkantha, Kathmandu (mail: P. O. Box 3520)/ Tel. +977 (01) 225087

Kuala Lumpur, Malaysia — Lot 9901, Jalan Awan Jawa, Taman Yarl, off 6½ Mile, Jalan Kelang Lama, Petaling/ Tel. +60 (03) 780-7355, -7360, or -7369

Manila, Philippines — 170 R. Fernandez, San Juan, Metro Manila/ Tel. +63 (02) 707410

Singapore — Govinda's Gifts, 763 Mountbatten Road, Singapore 1543/ Tel. +65 440-9092

Taipei, Taiwan — (mail: c/o ISKCON Hong Kong)

Tel Aviv, Israel — P. O. Box 48163, Tel Aviv 61480/ Tel. +972 (03) 5223718

Tokyo, Japan — 1-29-2-202 Izumi, Suginami-ku, Tokyo 168/ Tel. +81 (03) 3327-1541

Yogyakarta, Indonesia — P.O. Box 25, Babarsari YK, DIY

FARM COMMUNITIES

Indonesia — Govinda Kunja (contact ISKCON Jakarta)

Malaysia — Jalan Sungai Manik, 36000 Teluk Intan, Perak

Philippines (Hare Krishna Paradise) — 231 Pagsa-bungan Rd., Basak, Mandaue City/ Tel. +63 (032) 83254

ADDITIONAL RESTAURANTS

Cebu, Philippines — Govinda's, 26 Sanchiangko St.

Kuala Lumpur, Malaysia — Govinda's, 16-1 Jalan Bunus Enam, Masjid India/ Tel. +60 (03) 7807355 or 7807360 or 7807369

Singapore — Govinda's Restaurant, B1-19 Cuppage Plaza 5, Koek Rd., 0922/ Tel. +65 735-6755

LATIN AMERICA

BRAZIL

Belém, PA — Rua Lindolpho Collor, 42, Marco, CEP 66095-310

Belo Horizonte, MG — Rua Santo Antonio, 45, Venda Nova, CEP 31515-100

Brasilia, DF — HIGS 706, Bloco C, Casa 29, CEP 70350-752/ Tel. +55 (061) 242-7579

♦ **Caxias Do Sul, RS** — Rua Italia Travi, 601, Rio Branco, CEP 95097-710

Curitiba, PR — Comunidade Nova Goloka, Pinhais (Mail: R.Cel Anibal dos Santos 67, Vila Fanny, Curitiba, CEP 81030-210)

Florianopolis, SC — Rua Joao de Souza, 200, Praia do Santinho, CEP 88056-678
Fortaleza, CE — Rua Jose Lourenço, 2114, Aldeota, CEP 60115-288/ Tel. +55 (085) 266-1273
♦ **Guarulhos, SP** — Rua Dom Pedro II, 195, Centro, 3rd floor, CEP 07131-418/ Tel. +55 (011) 209-6669
Manaus, AM — Av. 7 de Setembro, 1559, Centro, CEP 69005-141/ Tel. +55 (092) 232-0202
Natal, RN — Av. Praia do Timbau, 2133, Ponta Negra, CEP 59894-588
Pirajui, SP — Estr. Pirajui-Estiva, Km 2, CEP 16600-000/ Tel. +55 (0142) 72-2309.
Porto Alegre, RS — Rua Tomas Flores, 331, Bonfim, CEP 90035-201
♦ **Recife, PE** — Rua Zenobio Lins, 70, Cordeiro, CEP 50711-300
Ribeirao, Preto — Rua dos Aliados, 155, Campos Eliseos, CEP 14080-570
Rio de Janeiro, RJ — Rua Armando C. de Freitas, 108, B. Tijuca, CEP 22628-098/ Tel. +55 (021) 399-4493
Salvador, BA — Rua Alvaro Adrono, 17, Brotas, CEP 40255-460/ Tel. +55 (071) 244-0418
Santos, SP — Rua Nabuco de Araujo, 151, Embare, CEP 11025-011/ Tel. +55 (0132) 38-4655
São Paulo, SP — Av. Angelica, 2583, Centro, CEP 01227-200/ Tel. +55 (011) 259-7352
Teresopolis, RJ — Comunidade Vrajabhumi (contact ISKCON Rio)

FARM COMMUNITIES
Caruaru, PE — Nova Vrajadhama, Distrito de Murici (mail: C.P. 283, CEP 55000-000)
Parati, RJ — Goura Vrindavana, Sertao Indaituba (mail: 62 Parati, CEP 23970-000)
Pindamonhangaba, SP — Nova Gokula, Bairro de Ribeirao Grande (mail: C.P. 108, CEP 12400-000)/ Tel. +55 (0122) 42-5002

ADDITIONAL RESTAURANT
Caxias do Sul, RS — Av. Julio de Castilhos, 1095, Centro

MEXICO
♦ **Guadalajara** — Pedro Moreno No. 1791, Sector Juarez/ Tel. +52 (36) 160775
Mexico City — Gob. Tiburcio Montiel No. 45, 11850 Mexico, D.F./ Tel. +52 (5) 271-22-23
Saltillo — Blvd. Saltillo No. 520, Col. Buenos Aires

FARM COMMUNITY
Guadalajara — Contact ISKCON Guadalajara

ADDITIONAL RESTAURANTS
Orizaba — Restaurante Radhe, Sur 5 No. 50, Orizaba, Ver./ Tel. +52 (272) 5-75-25
Tulancingo — Restaurante Govinda, Calle Juarez 213, Tulancingo, Hgo./ Tel. +52 (775) 3-51-53

PERU
Lima — Pasaje Solea 101 Santa Maria-Chosica/ Tel. +51 (014) 910891
♦ **Lima** — Schell 634 Miraflores

FARM COMMUNITY
Correo De Bella Vista — DPTO De San Martin

ADDITIONAL RESTAURANT
Cuzco — Espaderos 128
Lima — Av. Garcilazo de la Vega 1670-1680/ Tel. +51 (014) 259523

OTHER COUNTRIES
Asunción, Paraguay — Centro Bhaktivedanta, Paraguari 469, Asunción/ Tel. +595 (021) 492-800
Bogotá, Colombia — Carrera 16, No. 60-52, Bogota (mail: Apartado Aereo 58680, Zona 2, Chapinero)/ Tel. +57 (01) 2486892, 210665
Buenos Aires, Argentina — Centro Bhaktivedanta, Andonaegui 2054 (1431)/ Tel. +54 (01) 515567
Buenos Aires, Argentina — Gusto Superior, Blanco Encalada 2722, 1428 Buenos Aires, Capital Federal/ Tel. +54 (01) 7883025
Cali, Colombia — Avenida 2 EN, #24N-39/ Tel. +57 (023) 68-88-53
Caracas, Venezuela — Avenida Berlin, Quinta Tia Lola, La California Norte/ Tel. +58 (02) 225463
Chinandega, Nicaragua — Edificio Hare Krsna No. 108, Del Banco Nacional 10 mts. abajo/ Tel. +505 (341) 2359
Cochabamba, Bolivia — Av. Heroinas E-0435 Apt. 3 (mail: P. O. Box 2070)/ Tel. & Fax +591 (042) 54346
Essequibo Coast, Guyana — New Navadvipa Dham, Mainstay, Essequibo Coast
Georgetown, Guyana — 24 Uitvlugt Front, West Coast Demerara
Guatemala, Guatemala — Apartado Postal 1534
♦ **Guayaquil, Ecuador** — 6 de Marzo 226 or V. M. Rendon/ Tel. +593 (04) 308412 y 309420

♦ **Zürich** — Preyergrasse 16, 8001 Zürich/ Tel. +41 (1) 251-88-51

OTHER COUNTRIES

Amsterdam, The Netherlands — Van Hilligaertstraat 17, 1072 JX, Amsterdam/ Tel. +31 (020) 6751404

Antwerp, Belgium — Amerikalei 184, 2000 Antwerpen/ Tel. +32 (03) 237-0037

Athens, Greece — Methymnis 18, Kipseli, 11257 Athens/ Tel. +30 (01) 8658384

Barcelona, Spain — c/de L'Oblit 67, 08026 Barcelona/ Tel. +34 (93) 347-9933

Belgrade, Serbia — VVZ-Veda, Custendilska 17, 11000 Beograd/ Tel. +381 (11) 781-695

Budapest, Hungary — Hare Krishna Temple, Mariaremetei ut. 77, Budapest 1028 II/Tel. +36 (01) 1768774

Copenhagen, Denmark — Baunevej 23, 3400 Hillerød/ Tel. +45 42286446

Debrecen, Hungary — L. Hegyi Mihalyne, U62, Debrecen 4030/ Tel. +36 (052) 342-496

Helsinki, Finland — Ruoholahdenkatu 24 D (III krs) 00180, Helsinki/ Tel. +358 (0) 6949879

Iasi, Romania — Stradela Moara De Vint 72, 6600 Iasi

Kaunas, Lithuania — Savanoryu 37, Kaunas/ Tel. +370 (07) 222574

Klaipeda, Lithuania — Rumpiskes 14, 5802 Kleipeda/ Tel. +370 (061) 31735

Lisbon, Portugal — Rua Fernao Lopes, 6, Cascais 2750 (mail: Apartado 2489, Lisbo 1112)/ Tel. +351 (011) 286 713

Ljubljana, Slovenia — Zibertova 27, 61000 Ljubljana/ Tel. +386 (061) 131-23-19

Madrid, Spain — Espíritu Santo 19, 28004 Madrid/ Tel. +34 (91) 521-3096

Málaga, Spain — Ctra. Alora, 3 int., 29140 Churriana/ Tel. +34 (952) 621038

Oslo, Norway — Senter for Krishnabevissthet, Skolestien 11, 0373 Oslo 3/ Tel. +47 (022) 494790

Paris, France — 31 Rue Jean Vacquier, 93160 Noisy le Grand/ Tel. +33 (01) 43043263

Plovdiv, Bulgaria — ul. "Petyofi" 20, Plovdiv 4000/ Tel. +359 (032) 270392 or 270391

Porto, Portugal — Rua S. Miguel, 19 C.P. 4000 (mail: Apartado 4108, 4002 Porto Codex)/ Tel. +351 (02) 2005469

Prague, Czech Republic — Jilova 290, Prague 5-Zlicin 155 21/ Tel. +42 (02) 3021282 or 3021608

♦ **Riga, Latvia** — 56 Krishyana Barona, LV 1001/ Tel. +371 (02) 272490

Rotterdam, The Netherlands — Braamberg 45, 2905 BK Capelle a/d Yssel./ Tel. +31 (010) 4580873

Santa Cruz de Tenerife, Spain — C/ Castillo, 44, 4°, Santa Cruz 38003,Tenerife/ Tel. +34 (922) 241035

Sarajevo, Bosnia-Herzegovina — Saburina 11, 71000 Sarajevo/ Tel. +381 (071) 531-154

♦ **Septon-Durbuy, Belgium** — Chateau de Petite Somme, 6940 Septon-Durbuy/ Tel. +32 (086) 322926

Shyauliai, Lithuania — Vytauto 65a, 5408 Shyauliai/ Tel. +370 (014) 99323

Skopje, Macedonia — Vvz. "ISKCON," Roze Luksemburg 13, 91000 Skopje/ Tel. +389 (091) 201451

Sofia, Bulgaria — Neofit Rilski 31, Sofia 1000/ Tel. +359 (02) 814548

Sofia, Bulgaria — Villa 3, Vilna Zona-Iztok, Simeonovo, Sofia 1434/ Tel. +359 (02) 6352608

Timisoara, Romania — ISKCON, Porumbescu 92, 1900 Timisoara/ Tel. +40 (961) 54776

Turku, Finland — Kaurakatu 39, 20/40 Turku 74/ Tel. +358 (21) 364 055

♦ **Vienna, Austria** — Center for Vedic Studies, Rosenackerstrasse 26, 1170 Vienna/ Tel. +43 (01) 222455830

Vilnius, Lithuania — Raugyklos G. 23-1, 2056 Vilnius/ Tel. +370 (0122) 66-12-18

FARM COMMUNITIES

Czech Republic — Krsnuv Dvur c. 1, 257 28 Chotysany

Denmark — Gl. Kirikevej 3, 6650 Broerup/ Tel. +45 (075) 392921

France (Dole)— Chateau Bellevue, F-39700 Chatenois/ Tel. +33 84 72 82 35

France (La Nouvelle Mayapura) — Domaine d'Oublaisse, 36360, Lucay le Mâle/ Tel. +33 (054) 402481

Spain (New Vraja Mandala) — (Santa Clara) Brihuega, Guadalajara/ Tel. +34 (911) 280018

ADDITIONAL RESTAURANTS

Barcelona, Spain — Restaurante Govinda, Plaza de la Villa de Madrid 4–5, 08002 Barcelona

Copenhagen, Denmark — Govinda's, Noerre Farimagsgade 82/ Tel. +45 33337444

Prague, Czech Republic—Govinda, Na hrzai 5, Prague 8, Liben/ Tel +42 (02) 6837226

Prague, Czech Republic—Govinda, Soukenicka 27, Prague 1/Tel. +42 (02) 4816016

Managua, Nicaragua — Residencial Bolonia, De Galeria los Pipitos 75 mts. norte (mail: P.O. Box 772)/ Tel. +505 242759

Mar del Plata, Argentina — Dorrego 4019 (7600) Mar del Plata/ Tel. +54 (023) 745688

Mendoza, Argentina — Espejo 633, (5000) Mendoza/ Tel. +54 (061) 257193

Montevideo, Uruguay — Centro de Bhakti-Yoga, Pablo de Maria 1427, Montevideo/ Tel. +598 (02) 2484551

Panama, Republic of Panama — Via las Cumbres, entrada Villa Zaita, frente a INPSA No.1 (mail: P.O. Box 6-29-54, Panama)

Pereira, Colombia — Carrera 5a, #19-36

♦ **Quito, Ecuador** — Inglaterra y Amazonas

Rosario, Argentina — Centro de Bhakti-Yoga, Paraguay 556, (2000) Rosario/ Tel. +54 (041) 252630

San José, Costa Rica — Centro Cultural Govinda, Av. 7, Calles 1 y 3, 235 mtrs. norte del Banco Anglo, San Pedro (mail: Apdo. 166,1002)/ Tel. +506 23-52 38

San Salvador, El Salvador — Avenida Universitaria 1132, Media Quadra al sur de la Embajada Americana (mail: P.O. Box 1506)/ Tel. +503 25-96-17

Santiago, Chile — Carrera 330/ Tel. +56 (02) 698-8044

Santo Domingo, Dominican Republic — Calle Cayetano Rodriquez No. 254

Trinidad and Tobago, West Indies — Orion Drive, Debe/ Tel. +1 (809) 647-3165

Trinidad and Tobago, West Indies — Prabhupada Ave. Longdenville, Chaguanas

FARM COMMUNITIES

Argentina (Bhaktilata Puri) — Casilla de Correo No 77, 1727 Marcos Paz, Pcia. Bs.

As., Republica Argentina

Bolivia — Contact ISKCON Cochabamba

Colombia (Nueva Mathura) — Cruzero del Guali, Municipio de Caloto, Valle del Cauca/ Tel. 612688 en Cali

Costa Rica — Nueva Goloka Vrindavana, Carretera a Paraiso, de la entrada del Jardin Lancaster (por Calle Concava), 200 metros al sur (mano derecha) Cartago (mail: Apdo. 166, 1002)/ Tel. +506 51-6752

Ecuador (Nueva Mayapur) — Ayampe (near Guayaquil)

Ecuador (Giridharidesha) — Chordeleg (near Cuenca), Cassiga Postal 01.05.1811, Cuenca/ Tel. +593 (7) 255735

El Salvador — Carretera a Santa Ana, Km. 34, Canton Los Indios, Zapotitan, Dpto. de La Libertad

Guyana — Seawell Village, Corentyne, East Berbice

ADDITIONAL RESTAURANTS

Buenos Aires, Argentina — Gusto Superior, Blanco Encalada 2722, 1428 Buenos Aires Cap. Fed./ Tel. +54 (01) 788 3023

Cochabamba, Bolivia — Gopal Restaurant, calle España N-0250 (Galeria Olimpia) (mail: P. O. Box 2070, Cochabamba)/ Tel. +591 (042) 26626

Guatemala, Guatemala — Callejor Santandes a una cuadra abajo de Guatel, Panajachel Solola

San Salvador, El Salvador — 25 Avenida Norte 1132

Santa Cruz, Bolivia — Snack Govinda, Av. Argomosa (1ero anillo), esq. Bolivar/ Tel. +591 (03) 345189